Nearly Forgotten

Seventh-day Adventists in Jamaica, Vermont, and Their Place in Vermont History

This is the story about a group of people whose experience
reflected the discouragement of their origins,
the hope of their spiritual beliefs,
and the struggles of their mundane surroundings.

Floyd Greenleaf

TEACH Services, Inc.
P U B L I S H I N G
www.TEACHServices.com • (800) 367-1844

World rights reserved. This book or any portion thereof may not be copied or reproduced in any form or manner whatever, except as provided by law, without the written permission of the publisher, except by a reviewer who may quote brief passages in a review.

The author assumes full responsibility for the accuracy of all facts and quotations as cited in this book. The opinions expressed in this book are the author's personal views and interpretations, and do not necessarily reflect those of the publisher.

This book is provided with the understanding that the publisher is not engaged in giving spiritual, legal, medical, or other professional advice. If authoritative advice is needed, the reader should seek the counsel of a competent professional.

Copyright © 2017 Floyd Greenleaf

Copyright © 2017 TEACH Services, Inc.

ISBN-13: 978-1-4796-0344-2 (Paperback)

ISBN-13: 978-1-4796-0345-9 (ePub)

ISBN-13: 978-1-4796-0346-6 (Mobi)

Library of Congress Control Number: 2017904332

*To the memory of the people
who constituted the Seventh-day Adventist Church
in Jamaica, Vermont,
whose homespun roots and way of life
left a legacy of spiritual strength to their peers,
their community, and state.*

Table of Contents

Foreword 7
Introduction 9
Millerite Background: 1831–1844 19
Sabbatarian Adventism: the 1850s 30
Organization and the Meetinghouse in Jamaica: 1860–1875 35
A New Beginning with A. S. Hutchins: 1875–1885 45
Coming of Age: 1885–1895 56
Early Sabbatarian Adventist Families in Jamaica 65
Later Adventist Families 83
Decline and Demise 99
Retrospect 112
Bibliography 126

Credit: Jamaica Historical Foundation

A panorama of the village of Jamaica, Vermont, at an unknown date. The mountainous character of the region is clearly visible. The hamlet of Pikes Falls lies about five miles to the west of the village near the township line of Stratton.

Foreword

When was the last time you heard a discussion of the Adventist church in Jamaica, Vermont? Probably never. In fact, most people have never heard of the community itself.

So why write a history of this congregation, especially since it no longer exists? Its last church building has been sold and remodeled as a private home. All the denomination still owns related to this once thriving congregation is a small graveyard.

Yet the Jamaica/Pikes Falls church was at one time the largest congregation in Vermont and probably in the three states of northern New England. What happened? How did it "disappear"? What forces inside the congregation and in its surrounding community led to its rise and demise?

It is such questions that Floyd Greenleaf helpfully explores in his well-researched *Nearly Forgotten: Seventh-day Adventists in Jamaica, Vermont, and Their Place in Vermont History*. The subtitle highlights an important part of the book since the author demonstrates that a congregation's history is closely tied to that of its local community.

It can be argued that the Jamaican Adventist "failure" is the very reason why this history is important. All too often we gauge the importance of a historical topic in terms of success. But successes are only a part of the story. While the dynamics of growth and largeness are important to understand, so are those of smallness and demise. Both are crucial if we want to understand the history of any topic, including local congregations. As such, Greenleaf, as one of the foremost students of Adventist history, has performed a distinct service in devoting his talents to this local history.

It should be noted that small books are not at the forefront of Greenleaf's past as an author. One only has to think of his two-volume, 1,000-page, *Seventh-day Adventist Church in Latin America and the Caribbean* or his significant revision and expansion of the material on the South American Division under the title of *A Land of Hope* to recognize that Greenleaf is not a scholar of small things. The same can be said of his authorship of *In Passion for the World: A History of Seventh-day Adventist Education* or his significant revision and updating of Richard Schwarz's *Light-Bearers: A History of the Seventh-day Adventist Church*.

Greenleaf through his historical work has enabled us to see the big picture of denominational history along several lines. And now he has refocused and helped us begin to understand the "small" picture. It is my hope that this slim volume will be read with care because its lessons are important. Beyond that, it provides a model for other local histories yet to be written. Thus I would like to conclude this foreword with an invitation and a challenge to both professional historians and lay history buffs to not only become interested in local denominational history but to write out their findings. Many of those studies will probably never be published, but at the very least they should be entered into the electronic media and filed in an Adventist research center such as that found at Andrews University and increasingly in Adventist colleges and universities around the world. Every such study will enable us to better understand the church and its dynamics.

George R. Knight
Professor Emeritus of
Church History
Andrews University

Introduction

Jamaica, Vermont, is a rural township in Windham County on the southeastern slopes of the Green Mountains. Its largest settlement is Jamaica, which squats where the Ball Mountain Brook joins the larger West River as it pours from the hills and then meanders about twenty miles southeast beyond the village before emptying into the Connecticut River near Brattleboro. Several hamlets are scattered about the township. Perhaps the best known is Pikes Falls, which is also a region that begins at a point near the center of the west boundary of the township and extends into neighboring Stratton.

Jamaica's Background

The most plausible beginning point for Jamaica is a charter from the Independent Republic of Vermont in 1780 that authorized nearly seventy grantees to settle in the township. It is not possible to put a date on the moment when Jamaica lost its frontier character. The first settlers soon learned that they could not easily subdue the land. The area has always remained rough-hewn and its people unpretentious. On April 15, 1869, Isaac Pike, from whom Pikes Falls received its name, recorded in his diary that the temperature on that spring morning was 25˚F. Later that day he measured more than five feet of snow on the east side of nearby Stratton Mountain.[1]

When Helen and Scott Nearing moved to Pikes Falls in 1932, they entered a community that had no flush toilets and met children who had never tasted an ice cream soda. Some of them could hardly believe that coal was a combustible substance. The Nearings remarked that the young were "as removed from modern civilization as if they had been born in some remote Alpine village."[2] Helen and Scott found the elevation too high for successful fruit farming. They calculated the average frost-free growing season to be about eighty-five days, but actually, crops were vulnerable to frosts anytime. Killing frosts hit their gardens in June, July, and August of 1947. Commonly, they said, snow covered the ground from Thanksgiving to Easter. The Nearings once endured a foot of new snow in late May. Their most formidable problem was the climate.[3]

Common schools had long been a part of Jamaica's history, but agricultural needs shaped educational practices. Greg Joly has noted that school customarily closed for two weeks during the maple sugaring season to allow children to work the maple orchards and sugarhouses. Elizabeth Hurd Greene, who was born in Pikes Falls in 1927, recalled one season when the local school shut down for the entire month of March in deference to maple sugar production. She and her siblings had done most of the family sugaring, she remembered. A loss of a month or even two weeks would cut deeply into a school year, which was only sixteen to nineteen weeks in Pikes Falls as late as World War II.[4]

I became interested in Jamaica after discovering that I had genealogical ties with Pikes Falls. It was during an October afternoon in 2007 that Harold and Aina Lindquist from nearby West Townshend led my wife and me to the Pikes Falls Cemetery where, for the first time, I saw the grave of Joseph Dompier, one of my great-grandfathers. The search for his grave had occupied several months of scrutinizing records and following leads. Overgrowth covered the small cemetery and nearly obscured his broken headstone. His death in 1877 at the age of forty-three occurred after he and his family had lived in Pikes Falls for seven years.

The Dompiers attended the Seventh-day Adventist church in Jamaica. The old meetinghouse stood virtually in the shadow of Isaac Pike's sawmill and was known in Adventist circles as the Jamaica church. But by the twentieth century, the congregation more often went by the name of the Pikes Falls church.

Compelled by a growing curiosity, I searched for information about this church and the nook in the Green Mountains where my maternal grandmother spent her early childhood. Once organized, the facts constituted a tantalizing story, not only about the church itself but also how it fit into the broader history of the Seventh-day Adventist denomination and even the state of Vermont.

Reform, Unconventionality, and Religion

Vermont history is something less than a hot topic among American historians. One hindrance to people's perception of the state's importance is its small size. The 2010 census revealed that more than sixty urban areas in the United States exceeded the entire population of Vermont, which approximated 626,000 when the count took place.

But the state's history is not without intriguing moments. Before the end of the Revolutionary War, Vermont dissociated itself from the thirteen colonies and existed briefly as an independent republic. Vermont was the first territory to join the United States, becoming the fourteenth state in 1791. Near Vermont's shared border with Canada, an Anglo-French imbroglio erupted into warfare in 1837. Vermont could not avoid involvement in this fracas because of its proximity to the troubled region. Vermont experienced an immigration/emigration problem like few other states. Much like a teenager on the brink of proverbial fool's hill, Vermont also had its fling with extremism.

> *Much like a teenager on the brink of proverbial fool's hill, Vermont also had its fling with extremism.*

Paul Searls has argued that Vermont history is the record of a great ideological divide between the uphill and downhill people, which, he explains, is more than geographic ups and downs. It is a history of values espoused by the rural and conservative as opposed to the urban and progressive, or otherwise stated, tradition rivaled by modernity.[5]

However, historians have more often portrayed Vermont history as a contrasting record of East *vis-a-vis* West, the two regions separated by the Green Mountains that form the topographical spine of the state and divide the population both geographically and, they say, ideologically. The chief geographic features of these two regions are watersheds: first, the Connecticut River Valley in the east that runs from north to south the entire length of the state and separates it from New Hampshire, and second, the Lake Champlain basin that dominates the west.

Some students of Vermont's past claim that these two regions attracted settlers venturing northward from separate parts of lower New England and that their baggage included differences in mentality, political sentiment, and religious persuasion. The lines of demarcation were neither clean nor absolute, but the argument contends that the great mountain divide separated an East that tended to be more conservative from a West that was prone to change and dissent, and consequently, more separatist.

As these attitudes touched Christian practices, Calvinist thinking appeared stronger in the East, while western Vermonters were more willing to concede that individual will played a role in spiritual decision-making and the eternal destinies of human beings. The most extreme case in point was the movement of deism that cropped up in southwestern Vermont. Led by Ethan Allen during the era of the American Revolution, this intellectual mood rejected divine intervention in human experience, and for practical purposes, rejected religion altogether.

Jeffrey Potash has explained that the colonists' successful revolt against England unleashed a surge of Jeffersonian democracy that was cordial to deism. Thus, he states, Allen's adventure into philosophy was linked to wider political debates of the American early national period. In this scenario, eastern Vermont was more Federalist than the western part of the state.[6] Whatever the political implications of religious practice were, deism was an undisputed philosophical pole diametrically opposite from Calvinism's determinism that was more common in the east.

Less extreme than deism but more expressive of religious enthusiasm than Calvinism was the fire of nineteenth-century religious revival that spread across the state. This revival sometimes fluctuated with torrential power, especially in portions of west-central Vermont. Speaking from the vantage point that presupposes humans are free moral agents, preachers often thundered with holy vehemence to encourage listeners to decide their eternal fate, preferably one way rather than the other. Historians have called the area where these spiritual battles waxed hottest the "burned-over district."[7]

The image of a scorched land first appeared during the Second Great Awakening when Charles Grandison Finney applied the term to north-central New York State. There, the heat of repeated revivals left the countryside metaphorically burned and smoking.[8] Whitney Cross links this fervor to droves of settlers who relocated to upper New York after migrating westward from Vermont, particularly from the western side of the Green Mountains. Their new locations in New York provided fertile soil for farming as well as a spawning ground for colonies dedicated to religious experiments, such as perfectionism, communitarianism, and sometimes free-love, all under the umbrella of utopian-millennialist reform.[9]

Alice Felt Tyler lumps Vermont's burned-over district with New York's to constitute a single region of religious enthusiasm.[10] But we twenty-first-century spectators of history need to view cautiously the generalization that, in Jeff Crocombe's words, characterizes people in the burned-over regions of Vermont and New York as "predisposed to religious extremism."[11]

Readers should not infer from Crocombe's statement that religious enthusiasm and its kindred moods of reform and extremism were absent outside the burned-over regions. A predisposition is not an absolute, but rather a tendency that allows exceptions. Exceptions cropped up aplenty in Vermont because reform was an important element of postmillennialism, the reigning theology on both sides of the Green Mountains. A prime example occurred in Jamaica, lying south of the burned-over district within the Connecticut River watershed, where the first antislavery society organized in 1833.[12] By 1846, Searls writes, the abolition movement had spread across the entire state–every church in Vermont had condemned slavery.[13]

Justifying itself as reform, extremism also erupted outside the burned-over region. In 1836, fifteen miles east of Jamaica in Putney, practically on the banks of the Connecticut River, J. H. Noyes founded a colony devoted to perfectionism. Eleven years later, in 1847, he transferred his disciples to Oneida, New York. In its new location, this millennialist group generated even more notoriety as the Oneida Community, one of the most widely known utopian religious communities of the era.[14]

By the mid-nineteenth century, the urge for religious reform and the wave of religious enthusiasm in Vermont subsided, but a recognition prevailed that persons of an unconventional mindset had found a congenial atmosphere in the state and had left their stamp on its history. To celebrate Vermont's frolic with nonconformism, promoters of every movement from spiritism and universalism to women's rights and antislavery converged on Rutland for a three-day conference in 1858. During their rhetorical melee, this gathering of unlikely bedfellows fired salvo after salvo at one another as well as at the United States at large, all in the name of millennialist reform. Borrowing a line from a Portland, Maine, newspaper, Thomas L. Altherr has called the event a "convention of moral lunatics."[15]

The Rutland affair had little national impact, but it did not end Vermont's experience with unconventionality. Helen and Scott Nearing attracted international attention to their private campaign for self-sufficient living during their residence in Pikes Falls from 1932 to 1952. The Nearings pitted themselves against North American society, which, they believed, was disintegrating. Probably inspired by their example, at least a dozen other families moved to Pikes Falls during the 1940s to promote a cooperative rather than a competitive social order, blended with antiwar attitudes and nonviolent, subsistence living. In *Almost Utopia,* Greg Joly identifies three "intentional communities" in Pikes Falls during the 1940s and 1950s, each espousing differing aspects of nonconformism. In the end, their ideals could not survive the internal discord they had generated.[16]

Few will deny the claims of some historians that exuberance and less restraint were more common west of the Green Mountains than east of the divide. However, the entire state has long felt the impact of social and religious ferment.

To understand the happenings in Jamaica, we must also take into account the emigration wave that washed thousands of settlers and their succeeding generations from Vermont's communities and farms. The exodus became a national issue. The most common explanation for Vermont's loss of population has been that settlers quickly tired of the state's hillside soil, which proved to be less fertile than they had anticipated. After wearing it out, they moved away to flatter, richer terrain in the West.[17]

Historians differ about the causes for either immigration to or emigration from Vermont. They have shown that causality is a multifaceted issue. Whatever the various reasons for migration, the significance of demographic movement to this study is two-pronged: emigration reduced Vermont to one of the most slowly growing states in the nation, and this trend impacted Jamaica.

Some have linked Vermont's shifting currents of religion and demography to an apocalyptic mentality that pervaded the religious atmosphere in the state during the first half of the nineteenth century. It was, the argument goes, attributable to both natural and human-made disasters. Among the setbacks were such events as the unusually cold summer of 1816 and the Panic of 1837. Those with consciences smitten by their own dereliction became easy targets for revivalists who conveniently seized the opportunity to explain calamity as divine judgment and punishment.[18]

Adventism and Vermont History

This study concludes that the story of the Seventh-day Adventist Church in Jamaica reflects the social, demographic, and religious conditions that shaped Vermont's character. The Adventist congregation in Jamaica originated from religious fervor and foundered in part on the rocks of general economic decline. Influences within Seventh-day Adventism itself also contributed to the fortunes of the church.

> *The Adventist congregation in Jamaica originated from religious fervor and foundered in part on the rocks of general economic decline.*

The roots of Seventh-day Adventism penetrate deeply into Millerism, a movement that historians often portray as an extremist wing of the Second Great Awakening. But Millerism was more than that. Its undergirding theology was premillennialism that challenged the postmillenialist theology of the Awakening.

As the prevailing theology of Protestantism, postmillennialism held that Jesus would fulfill His promise to return to this earth after humans had reformed the world and lived a thousand years in harmony with the ideals of Christianity. In short, Protestantism taught that the advent of Jesus was more or less a reward to humans for reforming themselves and creating a society free from wrong. Thus, postmillennial thinking held that human nature, though not perfect, was perfectible. Regardless of whether nineteenth-century reform in America was motivated specifically by these theological assumptions, much of it took place against the background of the postmillennial beliefs that dominated Protestant thinking.

In contrast, Millerism taught that human perfection presupposed an impossibility because humans are inherently sinful. Their hope for salvation depended on their complete reliance on the atoning life and death of Jesus. The advent of Jesus, which would be a time of judgment for a sinful world, would precede the Millennium. Instead of being an era of Christian goodness, this thousand-year period would be part of the judgment imposed at the time of the second advent of Jesus. Although both pre- and postmillennialism were philosophical parts of the Second Great Awakening, they were poles apart.

After emerging from Millerism, the Seventh-day Adventist movement continued its message of a premillennial advent. But at the same time, Seventh-day Adventists instituted many reforms that postmillennial theology fostered. Among these were temperance and health reform. However, as premillennialists, Seventh-day Adventists did not connect their reforms to postmillennial theology. They saw their activities as more in keeping with cultivating a sense of personal responsibility for individual well-being and humanitarianism. They sought to emulate the example of Jesus, who spent much of His ministry responding to human needs. The importance that Seventh-day Adventists attached to their social programs also assumed a link to an overarching goal of global evangelism. The narrative that follows demonstrates that these varying influences were present in the Seventh-day Adventist Church in Jamaica.

Acknowledgments

To write this book I have depended on many people and sources. The idea originated with a cousin, Lucille Lockwood, who helped to track down genealogical facts that eventually led us to our great-grandfather's grave. Personnel at several libraries and archival collections of original sources lent me their assistance: Charlotte County Library, Port Charlotte, Florida; American-French Library, Woonsocket, Rhode Island; Center for Adventist Research, Andrews University, Berrien Springs, Michigan; McKee Library, Southern Adventist University, Collegedale, Tennessee; Vermont Historical Library, Barre, Vermont; Vermont Vital Records, Middlesex, Vermont; Archives, Statistics and Research, and the Ellen G. White Estate, both at the General Conference of Seventh-day Adventists, Silver Spring, Maryland; *La Maison de Nos Aïeux* (House of our Ancestors), Île d'Orléans, Quebec; and *Les Archives Nationales du Québec*, Montreal, Quebec.

Charles Marchant of the Vermont Old Cemetery Association provided valuable information, including the Isaac Pike Diary, one of my key sources. D. K. Young, town clerk of Stratton, Vermont, helped to sort out information about Pikes Falls. Bonnie West, Jamaica town clerk and her assistant, Sophia Sanderson, as well as their successors, Pat Meulemans, clerk, and Terri Bills Garland, assistant, opened Jamaica's town records for me. Karen Ameden, president of the Jamaica Historical Foundation, shared information and made old photos available to me.

Richard and Russell Pike, great-great-grandsons of Isaac Pike, helped with information and pictures of Jamaica and Pikes Falls. Elizabeth Hurd

Greene and Howard Hurd, siblings who lived in Pikes Falls and attended the Seventh-day Adventist Church as children, also recollected part of the story.

I have benefitted from the suggestions of three readers of this study: Brian Strayer, professor of history at Andrews University and a researcher and writer of Seventh-day Adventist history; George R. Knight, emeritus professor of church history, Seventh-day Adventist Theological Seminary, Andrews University; and local historian Greg Joly of Jamaica.

No matter how many details about Jamaica and the people who lived there that we can ferret out of the dusty past, we will always miss some items of interest and importance. To that extent, our knowledge will always be imperfect. But as I studied and wrote about Jamaica and Pikes Falls, I became increasingly conscious of the significance of seemingly small bits of information that could change the story. Each uncovered detail helps us to understand the legacy not only of this interesting corner of Vermont but also of the entire state as well.

Notes
1. Isaac Pike Diary, owned by Charles Marchant, West Townshend, VT. Hereafter, this source cited as the Pike Diary.
2. Helen and Scott Nearing, *The Good Life* (New York: Schocken Books, Inc., 1989), p. 18.
3. Ibid. pp. 91, 92, 174.
4. Greg Joly and Rebecca Lepkoff, *Almost Utopia: The Residents and Radicals of Pikes Falls, Vermont, 1950* (Barre, VT: Vermont Historical Society, 2008), pp. 10, 57. Joly wrote the text and Lepkoff provided the photography. Elizabeth Hurd Greene, telephone interview by Floyd Greenleaf, October 1, 2012.
5. Paul M. Searls, *Two Vermonts: Geography and Identity, 1865–1910* (Durham: University of New Hampshire Press, 2006).
6. P. Jeffrey Potash, *Vermont's Burned-Over District* (Brooklyn, NY: Carlson Publishing, Inc., 1991), p. 126.
7. Besides Potash's study, two other valuable discussions about the "burned-over district" are Alice Felt Tyler, *Freedom's Ferment* (Minneapolis: University of Minnesota Press, 1944). See p. 68; and David Ludlum, *Social Ferment in Vermont* (New York: Columbia University Press, 1939). See p. 15.
8. Michael Barkun, *Crucible of the Millennium* (Syracuse: Syracuse University Press, 1986), p. 3.

9. Whitney R. Cross, *The Burned-Over District* (Ithaca: Cornell University Press, 1950), pp. 14–18.
10. Tyler, *Freedom's Ferment*, p. 68.
11. Jeff Crocombe, "'A Feast of Reason,' The Roots of William Miller's Biblical Interpretation and Its influence on the Seventh-day Adventist Church" (PhD dissertation, University of Queensland, Australia, 1991), p. 88.
12. Ludlum, *Social Ferment*, p. 146.
13. Searls, *Two Vermonts*, p. 17.
14. Ludlum, *Social Ferment*, pp. 244–248.
15. Thomas L. Altherr, "'A Convention of 'Moral Lunatics': The Rutland, Vermont, Free Convention of 1858," *Vermont History* (Winter 2001), pp. 90–104.
16. Scott and Helen Nearing entertained hundreds of visitors at their Pikes Falls homestead. See Nearing, *The Good Life*, p. 358. The Nearings wrote several books about their experience with self-sufficient living. The most well-known book was *Living the Good Life* (Harborside, ME: Social Science Institute, 1954), reprinted by Schocken books. Also see the chapters "From Away" and "Coda" in Joly and Lepkoff, *Almost Utopia*.
17. Lewis Stilwell proposes the rocky soil explanation as the primary issue among several other causes for emigration. See his *Emigration From Vermont* (Montpelier: Vermont Historical Society, 1948), pp. 232, 233.
18. Barkun, *Crucible*, pp. 103–123.

Millerite Background: 1831–1844

The Seventh-day Adventist Church in Jamaica, Vermont, emerged from the Millerite movement of the 1830s and early 1840s that swept first across New England and New York, then as far west as Ohio and Michigan, and south to Virginia. At the center of this spiritual wave was William Miller, a farmer living in Low Hampton, New York, who had become a Baptist minister.

Miller abandoned his hayfields in favor of a pulpit because his study of Scripture produced an unshakeable conviction that the second advent of Christ would occur sometime about the year 1843. He began to preach in 1831, speaking first near his home in towns in New York and Vermont. Eventually, he appeared in several other states and the Eastern Townships of Canada. In Vermont, his speaking engagements took him more frequently to the central and northern parts of the state rather than to the southern part. There is no record that he ever visited Jamaica.[1]

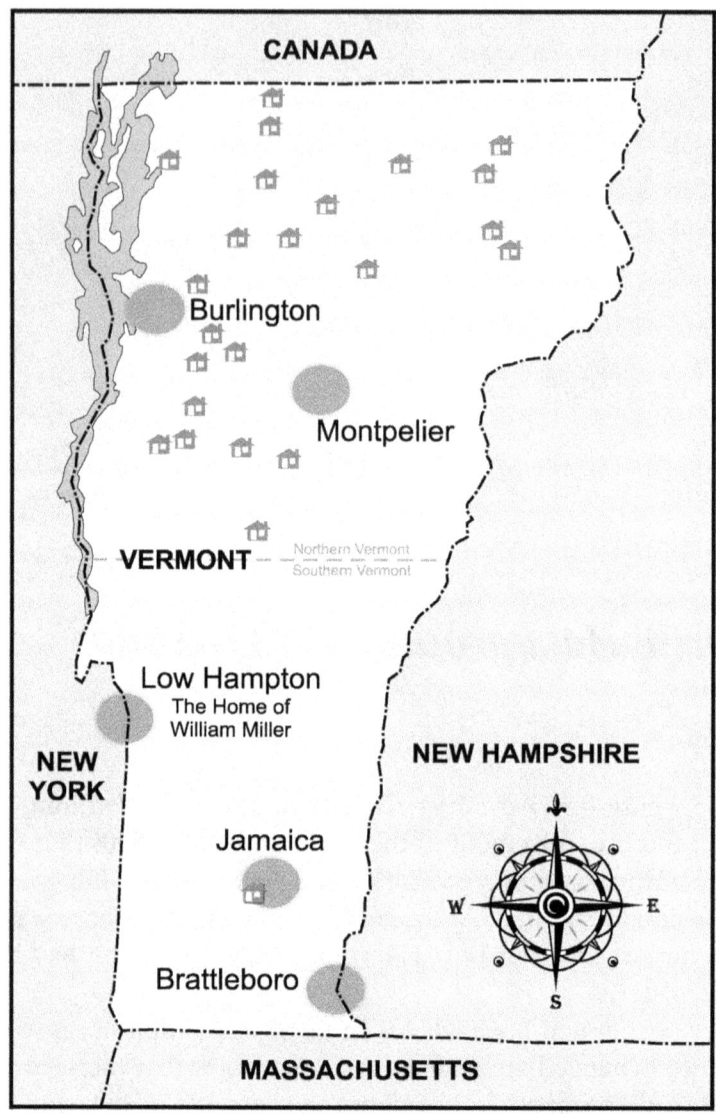

Note William Miller's home, Low Hampton, New York, about fifty miles northwest of Jamaica. Vermont is shown divided into north-south halves. The northern and southern boundaries are about eighty miles from the middle of the state. Icons indicate communities in which Seventh-day Adventists lived who attended the camp meeting of 1875. Their location in the northwestern quadrant reflects the strength of the Millerite movement in Vermont. Adventists in Jamaica were the only concentration of members in southern Vermont. See the chapter, "A New Beginning with A. S. Hutchins," for a discussion of these conditions.

William Miller's Preaching and Public Reaction

Early on, whether ministers concurred or disagreed with Miller's premillennial interpretation of the second advent, they invited him to their churches because listeners were curious about his ideas. His lectures also awakened spiritually drowsy congregations. Pastors saw him more as an effective revivalist than a bearer of an apocalyptic warning and impending judgment from heaven.[2] In Essex, Vermont, for example, presentations by Miller and two other speakers during 1839 and 1840 produced at least sixteen converts. During the same period, nearly sixty joined the Baptist church in Colchester after Miller delivered two series of lectures.[3]

By 1842, however, a growing number of churchmen saw Millerism as a schismatic, if not a destructive, force. T. M. Merriam described the second advent movement as the "gale of Millerism" that blew across the region of Johnson in northern Vermont.[4] Henry Crocker complained that Miller's lectures in Bennington in 1842 "wrought havoc in the flock."[5] Bennington's *State Banner* called Miller a monomaniac.[6] From Putney, Vermont, J. H. Noyes's *The Perfectionist* repeatedly hammered Miller with rebuttals to his message of a literal second advent. In August 1844, Noyes appealed to Millerites to confess that the "keystone of their prophetic arch has fallen."[7] Twenty-nine Baptist churches in Vermont evaporated between 1840 and 1849. Crocker suggested several causes for this loss, but he pinned most of the blame on Millerism, which, he said, "swept like a desolating fire" across the state.[8]

However, many reacted only casually to this heat. Gurdon Hibbard, a farmer near Chelsea, Vermont, who regularly attended the local Methodist meetinghouse, noted laconically in his diary that Sunday, June 18, 1843, was a pleasant day, and that he had visited a nearby Millerite camp meeting. Apparently, the appeal to prepare for the return of Jesus did not impress him with a sense of urgency. If he went back to hear more, he did not say so. But nonchalance was Hibbard's typical response to all Sunday sermons. His diary entries indicate that he listened to many of them—but without comment, except to recognize who preached.[9] Despite the gales and desolating fires throughout the state, there were throngs of Gurdon Hibbards in Vermont.

Critics may have decried Millerism, and casual listeners may have remained stoical, but many were convinced that they were hearing the truth and accepted Miller's explanations of biblical prophecy. By 1843, friction between the Millerites and their spiritual peers became incendiary. Crocker believed that the Millerites were out of control. He charged that they rejected those who did not adopt their views. To indict Millerites with their own phrases, Crocker quoted them as calling the churches of the day "Babalon" [sic] and "the mother of harlots," as well as an "abomination of the earth."[10] Those on the receiving end of this name-calling heard it as heresy, made worse by language that was biblical and apocalyptic.

Leaders of many churches disfellowshipped Millerites.[11] Sometimes the excommunicated were denied a chance to defend themselves, but on other occasions, they chose to leave. Churches in Jamaica closed their doors to people who believed in the second advent, who then met in a grove south of the village. In Grafton, less than a dozen miles from Jamaica, Millerites made it clear that separation from their churches was obligatory.[12] Speaking about cutting Millerites off, Crocker recalled that "they desired to be separated from the churches" and that "their exclusion was a necessity."[13]

Most Millerites reacted ambivalently to excommunication, relieved that they were no longer part of Babylon but at the same time feeling victimized. The public ridiculed them as fanatics, accusing them of causing lunacy, blaming them for inducing suicides, and mockingly alleging that they prepared ascension robes for the day of Christ's appearing.

During the era of the Second Great Awakening many preachers viewed religion as a celebration of fire and brimstone that consumed the wicked. Whitney Cross cites the greatest revivalist of the era, Charles Grandison Finney, as appealing to the Lord to "shake them off their seats" and to "shake them over hell," hardly language intended to soothe hearers. Although Finney was probably less noisy than many other clerics of his time, he set a tone for powerful preaching that lesser lights enthusiastically mimicked.[14] Sensationalism was common.

Millerism and Extremism

Millerites readily conceded that fanaticism erupted among their ranks, but all the responsibility did not rest on overly zealous preachers who incited extremist reactions. Some emotionally inclined listeners needed little or no prodding to adopt strange ideas and to lapse into a high-pitched fervor. Sixty years after the Millerite movement ended, George I. Butler recalled that "scores" of fanatics had gravitated to his father's house in Waterbury, Vermont. Young Butler, at the time a teenager, said he had a "schooling" in fanaticism, but his father sent the extremists "whirling."[15]

Although Millerites acknowledged outbursts of fanaticism among them, they drew the line at allegations that they caused lunacy and wore ascension robes. Despite their denials, the stories persisted. Some well-recognized historians have depicted Millerism as an exercise of madness,[16] but Miller discouraged fanaticism. Writing from Castleton, Vermont, in 1843 after a tour in Massachusetts, he expressed pain because some of his adherents exhibited "a proneness to wild and foolish extremes and vain delusions, such as working miracles, discerning of spirits, vague and loose views on sanctification, &c." To protect himself from the criticism of being fanatical, he sought to ground his preaching on Scripture alone.[17] Before his conversion, Miller had been an avowed deist. He formed his beliefs about the second advent by studying Scripture with a typical deist commitment to reason. Although he abandoned deism years before he ventured into the pulpit, to his death he continued to approach both Bible study and spirituality with a rationality that was rare among the clergy of the Second Great Awakening. Jeff Crocombe has concluded that Miller's systematic study of Scripture was rooted in the intellectual traditions of the Enlightenment, a "feast of reason," to use Miller's phrase, that still exerts an influence on Adventism.[18]

Regarding the hysteria, Gary Wait has wryly observed that no one wanted to spoil the stories of excesses by looking at the facts.[19] His remark represents a trend in scholarship—tempered by time, since it began in the nineteenth century—that defines much of the contemporary journalism as exaggeration, "gleefully" written and published, Ruth Alden Doan notes.[20] Students of the period have seen how easy it was for a sensationalist press to take advantage of an emotionally charged public. All too often, the label of insanity during the 1840s derived from popular opinion and was seasoned liberally with excitement. Such a diagnosis does not square well with twenty-first century understanding of mental illness. Historians acknowledge that clinicians, not street talk, define insanity. Researchers who have scrutinized the records of insane asylums operating during the 1840s are less convinced than nineteenth-century newspaper editors about insanity attributed to Millerism.[21]

All too often, the label of insanity during the 1840s derived from popular opinion and was seasoned liberally with excitement.

Regarding stories about ascension robes, two recent Vermont historians have reached opposite conclusions, the first stating that some

Millerites "fashioned paper or cloth wings" to expedite their flight upward; the second admitting the scarcity of "firsthand evidence" to support rumors about the robes.[22] Those who have delved into Millerism itself are persuaded that stories about ascension robes have no foundation. Third party accounts have been as close as anyone can get when trying to substantiate an allegation. "No conclusive evidence exists one way or the other," David Rowe declares.[23]

Such was the setting for the band of Millerites that sprouted up in Jamaica, Vermont, in 1842. Millerism was on the cusp of its troubled and painful years when a Millerite minister by the name of Chandler preached in this rural village about fifty miles southeast of Miller's home. Other revivalists followed.[24] According to commonly repeated accounts, these Millerite firebrands did their work well, both in attracting a following and stirring up ill will. These new Millerites in Jamaica did not escape the religious enthusiasm that also marked the gatherings of some other similarly convinced believers. Whether in Jamaica itself or in the general region is not clear, but authorities attempted to break up their meetings by jailing Stephen Pratt, an avid Millerite.[25]

As the time of the predicted advent neared, Millerites in Jamaica congregated in the farmhouse of Ira Young, who lived south of the village. J. D. Eddy recounts that the believers were "exhausted by fatigue, anxiety and, want of sleep" after conducting incessant meetings. Town authorities tried unsuccessfully to calm the situation. Within a few days, Mrs. Young died.[26]

The Midnight Cry, a Millerite publication, put a different twist on these events. Mrs. Young's death occurred only one week before October 22, 1844, the day when Millerite preachers finally agreed the second advent would occur. The faithful had gathered to pray for Mrs. Young's resurrection, believing that she should return to life "and remain with them till the Lord should appear." The *Midnight Cry* complained that the local justice of the peace hastily assembled a jury of inquest that crashed into the Youngs' house, accompanied by an excited crowd bent on quick justice. The upshot was a charge against Ira Young for poisoning his wife. The charge also included other Millerites who had gathered to pray for her resurrection. But the case ended abruptly when the coroner ruled that over-excitement was the cause of Mrs. Young's death.[27] The public tended to incriminate Millerism.

Local lore also blamed Millerite hysteria for a suicide by a Mrs. Stocker in Jamaica. Further, stories had it that on the long-looked-for day of the second advent, the faithful in Jamaica gathered on a hill—Greg Joly has identified the spot as The Pinnacle, west of the village—to await their translation to heaven. According to the oft-repeated account, the expectant believers garbed themselves in ascension robes and carried baskets to make it easy for descending angels to scoop up their children to begin their flight to paradise.[28]

Leading up to that day, Millerites could do little to assuage the angry locals, who were experiencing more excitement than they wanted. Their small community had acquired a reputation for fanaticism that historians would cite for generations to come as evidence of Millerite excess. Of course, the residents of Jamaica could not foresee the notoriety they had earned, but disgusted scoffers stoned and shot at Ira Young's house. The *Midnight Cry* alleged that members from some of the local churches broke into the Youngs' house and "applied a powerful dose of hartshorn to the noses of the brethren whilst engaged in prayer."[29]

Millerism was an interdenominational movement. Adherents came from many different communions, which meant that they understood the second advent against differing religious backgrounds. David Rowe describes the movement as having "little consensus of belief or practice . . . rife with disputes and contradictions. No coherent Millerite personality existed at all."[30] It was their common belief in the return of Jesus that bound them together.

After nothing happened on the appointed day, despair replaced the believers' hope. Recovery became their primary concern. Some returned to their original congregations. Others rejected the notion of a literal advent or turned away from religion altogether. The movement splintered badly and spawned a circle of new, small groups. Michael Barkun declares that hundreds joined the Shakers in the burned-over district of New York.[31] A few continued to believe in the second advent but with different shades of meaning about the advent itself.

Only a smattering held to their conviction that Miller's prophetic calculations had been correct but that the event they had predicted was wrong. Living in and around Jamaica, Vermont, after the Great Disappointment, a few of this last category of bewildered Millerites were groping for explanations.[32] It was on this uncertain and shaky foundation that the Seventh-day Adventist Church in Jamaica would rise.

Notes

1. Sylvester Bliss, *Memoirs of William Miller* (Boston: Joshua V. Himes, 1853). Bliss does not provide a complete list of the communities in which Miller spoke, but readers who plot Miller's travels will find more speaking appointments in the northern half of Vermont than in the southern half.
2. David L. Rowe, *Thunder and Trumpets* (Chico. CA: Scholars Press, 1985), p. 24.
3. L. C. Eddy, "Essex," in *Vermont Historical Gazetteer*, vol. 1 (Burlington, VT: A. M. Hemenway, 1867), p. 788. Henry Crocker, *History of the Baptists in Vermont* (Bellows Falls, VT: P. H. Gobie Press, 1913), p. 368. The latter notes that Miller's appearance in Essex started an increase of about fifty members. For Miller's experience in Colchester, see ibid., p. 378. Hereafter the *Vermont Historical Gazetteer* is abbreviated to *VHG*. The publication data differ from one volume to the next.
4. T. M. Merriam, "Johnson," in *VHG*, vol. 2, p. 678.
5. Crocker, *Baptists in Vermont*, p. 103.
6. Bennington *State Banner*, cited in the Burlington *Free Press*, February 17, 1843.
7. *The Perfectionist*, August 10, 1844. For examples of Noyes's comments, see copies for April 1, 1843, May 2, 1843, and November 2, 1844.
8. Crocker, *Baptists in Vermont*, pp. 460, 461.
9. Gurdon Hibbard, "Farm Diary and Account Book," Vermont Historical Library, Barre, Vermont.
10. Cited in Crocker, *Baptists in Vermont*, p. 124.
11. Ibid., pp. 145, 147, 376. For an absorbing account of Millerites coming out of Babylon, see George R. Knight, *Millennial Fever and the End of the World* (Nampa, ID: Pacific Press Publishing Association, 1993), pp. 141–158.
12. Donal Ward, "Religious Enthusiasm in Vermont, 1761–1847" (PhD dissertation, Notre Dame University, 1980), pp. 248, 249.
13. Crocker, *Baptists in Vermont*, p. 124.
14. Cross, *Burned Over*, p. 174. Concerning sensational rather than rational preaching, see the entire chapter, "New Measures," pp. 173–184.
15. George I. Butler to Ellen G. White, January 28, 1904, Ellen G. White Estate, General Conference of Seventh-day Adventists, Silver Spring, MD.
16. John Bach McMaster, *A History of the People of the United States, From the Revolution to the Civil War*, vol. 7 (New York: D. Appleton and Company, 1920), pp. 134–141; Clara Endicott Sears, *Days of Delusion*

(Boston: Houghton Mifflin Company, 1924). Chapters 9 and 10 focus on fanaticism; Ludlum, *Social Ferment*, pp. 250–260; Tyler, *Freedom's Ferment*, pp. 75–77. In his introduction to *Thunder and Trumpets*, David Rowe explains that the "truth about Millerism lies somewhere between the lurid descriptions of scoffers and the hagiographics of defenders."

17. Bliss, *Memoirs of William Miller*, p. 235. See the entire passage treating the issue of fanaticism, pp. 227–239. Tyler, *Freedom's Ferment*, p. 75. Even Clara Endicott Sears, who wrote one of the most widely read and cited indictments of Millerism, called Miller a "truly earnest and devout man." See the introduction in her *Days of Delusion*.
18. Bliss, *Memoirs of William Miller*, p. 77; see also Crocombe, "Feast of Reason."
19. Gary E. Wait, "The End of the World," *Dartmouth College Library Bulletin* (November 1993), p. 7. http://1ref.us/he (accessed April 8, 2012).
20. Ruth Alden Doan, *Miller Heresy, Millennialism, and American Culture* (Philadelphia: Temple University Press, 1987), p. 60.
21. Ibid., pp. 158–174. Also see Cross, *Burned Over*, p. 306; Rowe, *Thunder and Trumpets*, pp. 102, 103; Ronald L. Numbers and Janet S. Numbers, "Millerism and Madness: A Study of 'Religious Insanity' in Nineteenth-Century America," in Ronald L. Numbers and Jonathan M. Butler, eds., *The Disappointed* (Knoxville: University of Tennessee Press, 1993), pp. 92–117; Barkun, *Crucible*, p. 41. Gary Land has summarized succinctly the issue of fanaticism among Millerites in "The Historians and the Millerites: An Historiographical Essay," an introductory chapter to Everett N. Dick, *William Miller and the Advent Crisis* (Berrien Springs, MI: Andrews University Press, 1994), pp. xiii–xxvii.
22. See Randolph A. Roth, *The Democratic Dilemma* (Cambridge: Cambridge University Press, 1987), p. 218; and T. D. Seymour Bassett, *The Gods of the Hills* (Montpelier: Vermont Historical Society, 2000), p. 145.
23. Rowe, *Thunder and Trumpets*, p. 102. See Doan, *Miller Heresy*, pp. 60, 61, 185, 217, 242, n. 17. Some examples of writers who put the accusation of ascension robes in perspective or rejected it outright are Jane Marsh Parker, "Did the Millerites Have Ascension Robes?" *The Outlook* (October 13, 1894), pp. 582, 583; John Francis Sprague, "The Millerites in Maine," *Sprague's Journal of Maine History* (January/February/March 1922), pp. 1–6; F. D. Nichol, *The Midnight Cry* (Washington, D.C.: Review and Herald Publishing Association, 1944),

pp. 370–398; Cross, *Burned Over,* pp. 301, 301, 305, 306. Novelist and writer Jane Marsh Parker was the daughter of a Millerite preacher and wrote from personal experience. Nichol's study is apologetic in tone, but his scholarship is nevertheless convincing.
24. Eddy, "Millerism," *VHG*, vol. 5, p. 427. Although Millerism may not have arrived in Jamaica until 1842, Millerites had preached in the general region since 1838. Luther Boutelle, who preached in Londonderry, said that the second advent was a burning issue for miles around. See Luther Boutelle, *Sketch of the Life and Religious Experience of Eld. Luther Boutelle* (Boston: Advent Christian Publication Society, 1891), pp. 45–55.
25. "Aged Pilgrims," *Atlantic Union Gleaner*, March 30, 1904. This Seventh-day Adventist publication is the official organ of the Atlantic Union Conference, a union of conferences of churches in the northeastern United States formed in 1901. Hereafter this source cited as *Gleaner*.
26. See Eddy, "Millerism," in *VHG*, vol. 5, p. 427. More recent accounts have depended on Eddy's story. See Mark Worthen, *Hometown Jamaica* (Brattleboro, VT: Griswold Offset Printing, Inc., 1976), pp. 19, 20; Warren E. Booker, ed., *Historical Notes: Jamaica, Windham County, Vermont* (Brattleboro, VT: E. L. Hildreth & Co., 1940), pp. 41, 42.
27. *The Midnight Cry*, Dec. 12, 1844, cited in Ludlum, *Social Ferment*, pp. 257, 258; Rowe, *Thunder and Trumpets*, pp., 64, 65; and in Ward, "Religious Enthusiasm," p. 250. The *Midnight Cry* was a Millerite periodical published by Joshua V. Himes, 1842–1845.
28. Eddy, "Millerism," *VHG*, vol. 5, p. 427; Worthen, *Hometown Jamaica*, pp. 19, 20; Joly and Lepkoff, *Almost Utopia*, p.14.
29. *The Midnight Cry*, Dec. 12, 1844, cited in Ludlum, *Social Ferment*, pp. 256, 257, and Dick, *Miller and Crisis*, p. 157. Hartshorn was ammonia extracted from the antler of a hart.
30. Rowe, Thunder and Trumpets, p. x.
31. Barkun, *Crucible*, p. 96. See also Cross, *Burned Over,* p. 263.
32. For an example of how this last group of Vermonters felt about their experience of excommunication and disappointment, see a five-part memoir by Washington Morse of Brookfield, Vermont, who sat through two series of Miller's lectures. "Items of Advent Experience during the Past Fifty Years," *The Advent Review and Sabbath Herald,* September 11 through October 23, 1888. Especially relevant are Part 3, September 25, and Part 4, October 16. Hereafter this source cited

as *RH*. Morse wrote in Part 3: "After the final disappointment in the autumn of 1844, the many thousands who had embraced the message of the close of time and the coming of Christ, were greatly perplexed to understand that wonderful movement. They could not find it in their hearts to renounce it as not in the order of God, and they were certain that they had been sincere in their adherence to the cause they had espoused . . . I fully believe that it is the will of God, that we should not cast away the confidence that was had in that movement by those who were in it; but that we should cherish it, knowing that our work was in the order of God." For accounts about Millerism developing into the Advent Christian denomination, see Boutelle, *Sketch of Life and Experience*, and Isaac C. Wellcome, *History of the Second Advent Message and Mission, Doctrine and People* (Yarmouth, ME: I. C. Wellcome, 1874).

Sabbatarian Adventism: the 1850s

Led by Joseph Bates from Fairhaven, Massachusetts, and James and Ellen White from Maine, a small number of Adventists who clung to Miller's prophetic calculations came to be known as Sabbatarians, because after 1846 they taught Saturday, the seventh-day Sabbath, as a fundamental belief. By 1850, they added to their core beliefs new views of God's judgment, conditional immortality, and the theological and symbolic significance of the Old Testament sanctuary. Sabbatarians did not constitute a separate denomination, because they were so few and reluctant to organize. The glue that held them together was the strong personalities of Bates and the Whites. Very influential also was *The Advent Review and Sabbath Herald*, popularly called the *Review and Herald,* or more often, simply the *Review*, a paper that James White launched in 1850. He sent it to Adventists of any stripe.

By 1850, the Whites and Bates had toured parts of central and northern Vermont, lending moral support to scattered groups of Adventists and explaining Sabbatarianism and other doctrines. Not until the spring of 1852 did a Sabbatarian minister visit Jamaica. Months later Jamaica resident

Betsey E. Sage was still overwhelmed with the inspiration of that occasion. James White published part of her letter to him verbatim in the *Review*.

"When Brn. Wheeler and Day came here last spring [1852]," she wrote, "they found us in darkness with regard to the message; but since embracing it, we have enjoyed some of the sweet spirit of the holy Sabbath of the Lord our God, more than we did in keeping the first day of the week." Betsey was a reader of White's *Review*, and she confessed that she wept as she read letters that other Sabbatarians had written to the editor. Like most Sabbatarians of the time, she believed that the second advent for which she was waiting was imminent. "I cannot refrain from . . . giving glory to God for the free spirit of love that flows in my heart to all the saints scattered abroad, in the patient waiting time, keeping the commandments of God, and the faith of Jesus," she said, borrowing phraseology from Revelation.[1]

"Sister Sage," as James White called her in typically pastoral rhetoric, hinted strongly that Sabbatarian Adventists in Jamaica would welcome a minister to conduct more meetings. Frederick Wheeler, who had whetted her appetite for more discussion, was the pastor of a Sabbatarian congregation in Washington, New Hampshire, who became one of the first Millerite ministers to adopt the Saturday Sabbath. During much of the 1850s, he continued to visit scattered groups of Adventists, including the community in Jamaica.[2] But it was Joseph Bates instead of Wheeler who fulfilled Betsey Sage's request in May 1853.

"In this rocky, mountainous, uncultivated section of Vermont, we spent several days," Bates reported, "visiting and holding meetings with the scattered families who had embraced the message of the third angel, under the ministration of Brn. Wheeler and Day." Bates characterized the Adventists in Jamaica as "poor children . . . famishing for the truth in the last message of mercy." He left Jamaica, convinced that his trip had been worth his time and effort. The heads of four families had converted to Sabbatarianism, and he had baptized eleven.[3]

Among Bates's listeners was Isaac Newton Pike, the most prominent resident of Pikes Falls. But he was neither one of the baptized nor an immediate convert. Later his relatives labeled him a Millerite, but by his own account, he had "no desire to meddle with the doctrine of Adventists" and did not care about a Sabbath of any kind until Bates's arrival in Jamaica to lecture on the topic.

Pike's curiosity was piqued, but for nearly two years he mulled it over, reading the Bible through three times to search for information about Sabbath observance. The third reading convinced him that Bates had been right. "I have made that [Saturday] the day of rest for more than a year and a half," he wrote in 1857, "and feel to praise God that he has shown me the truth."[4] He later told Uriah Smith, then editor of the *Review*, that he had been in a "backslidden state" for thirty-five years before finally accepting the seventh-day Sabbath. Since that time, he said, "a flood of light has flown in upon my soul that I never saw before."[5]

Pike's relatives were stretching the facts when they called him a Millerite. The second advent had been the heart of the Millerite movement. Millerites ignored the issue of the Saturday Sabbath. Pike adopted both beliefs, but not until more than a decade after the Great Disappointment in 1844. By the time Pike converted, Millerism as a movement had long since become defunct, but according to the mood of the day, anyone believing in the second advent was a Millerite, irrespective of other religious practices or whether the individual had been part of the Millerite movement. If we choose to call Pike a Millerite, we must bear in mind that he was of the post-1844 variety rather than a Millerite such as was Betsey Sage, who had been a participant in the movement itself.

The decade of the 1850s was not an easy time for the Sabbatarians in Jamaica. Living in southern Vermont, they were quite distant from larger and more numerous clusters of seventh-day Sabbath keepers in the northern part of the state. It was easy for Sabbatarian ministers to neglect them. But Betsey Sage's letter and her invitation that led to Bates's meetings had gotten the attention of Sabbatarian leaders. From this point on they included Jamaica on their list of places in Vermont to visit. They soon added Vernon to their itineraries, a town about thirty miles from Jamaica in the southeast corner of the state, where another group of Sabbatarians lived.[6] But clergy were scarce. They made their rounds infrequently, and Jamaica was still not a priority on their agenda.

Perhaps few others than Stephen Pratt sensed how difficult Jamaica was. In 1854, a year after Joseph Bates had followed up on Frederick Wheeler's introduction of Sabbatarian beliefs to southern Vermont, Pratt wrote to James White from Jamaica, expressing the hope that another of the Lord's "faithful and qualified servants could come and spend a few days with us." About a decade had passed since Pratt's fired-up zeal for Millerism had landed him in jail. With an oblique allusion to Jamaica's unwanted notoriety as a cradle of fanaticism, he reminded White that prevailing attitudes in the community would not encourage visiting Sabbatarian ministers. It had been "a very stronghold of Adventism," Pratt remembered, implying that the strength of Sunday-observing Adventists had made Sabbatarianism a difficult way of life in Jamaica.[7]

Two years passed until 1856 when C. W. Sperry and H. B. Buck fulfilled Pratt's request for a visiting preacher. The pair arrived in Jamaica not only to encourage the Sabbatarians but also to bring a formal evangelistic series to the community. Pitching a tent for their meetings, they attracted several kinds of Adventists and two Sunday-keeping Adventist preachers. During the second day of the gathering, an argument broke out about which day of the week was the legitimate biblical Sabbath. For three days the debate went on, halting only after rowdies flattened the tent by cutting its ropes in several places and slashing its roof and walls. Workers spent a day-and-a-half repairing the damage.

The outrage was a blessing in disguise. Believing that the mischief makers had resorted to vandalism, the community turned its sympathy in favor of the visiting preachers. Chastened by public sentiment, even the culprits volunteered to guard the evangelistic premises at night. After the tent went back up, heavy rains set in, but inclement weather did not prevent a better-than-expected attendance the following Sunday. The audience sat for seven hours listening to lectures on the book of Revelation. All the trouble for the visiting speakers faded away when a prominent "Advent man" stood to confess his belief in what he had heard, and encouraged others to join him. Sperry and Buck did not identify this individual, but they wrote that they had a "refreshing season."[8]

Instead of one all-consuming doctrine, Sabbatarians discovered several related teachings that formed a kind of theological infrastructure.

For the Sabbatarians in general, not only in Jamaica, the decade of the 1850s was a time when they rediscovered their spiritual purposes. They were only one of several surviving strands of the Millerite movement that continued to perpetuate a belief in the second advent. But the Sabbatarian movement morphed into something more comprehensive than Millerism. C. Mervyn Maxwell concludes that the fervor that had swept Millerites so dramatically to the Great Disappointment brought unforeseen blessings. "The dark cloud of 1844 had a silver lining so bright that we can speak of it as 'the magnificent disappointment,'" he wrote.[9] Instead of one all-consuming doctrine, Sabbatarians discovered several related teachings that formed a kind of theological infrastructure. Pike alluded to this schema in his letter to *Review* editor Uriah Smith when he described his new understandings as a "flood of light" that he had not seen before.[10] Although the seventh-day Sabbath became the signature doctrine of the Sabbatarians, it shared its centrality with a continuing belief in the second advent. For the group in Jamaica as well as fellow Sabbatarians elsewhere, the 1850s was a formative decade.

Notes

1. "From Sister Sage," *RH*, January 20, 1853.
2. "Wheeler, Frederick," *Seventh-day Adventist Encyclopedia*, 2nd rev. ed., vol. M–Z, p. 871. Hereafter this source is cited as *SDA Encyclopedia*.
3. "From Bro. Bates," *RH*, July 7, 1853. Bates's term, "message of the third angel," is an allusion to the third angel of Revelation 14, which Sabbatarians often used metaphorically to describe their beliefs. The angel's message concludes with a reference to the saints who keep the commandments of God, which Sabbatarians taught included the seventh-day Sabbath commandment of the Decalogue.
4. Letter, I. N. Pike to *Advent Review and Sabbath Herald*, n.d., quoted in *RH*, March 12, 1857.
5. Letter, I. N. Pike to Bro. Smith, n.d., quoted in *RH*, April 23, 1857.
6. See notices for pastoral visits published in *RH*, November 21, 1854, and May 5, 1859.
7. "From Bro. Pratt," *RH*, March 21, 1854.
8. "Tent Meeting in Jamaica, Vt.," *RH*, September 25, 1856.
9. C. Mervyn Maxwell, *Magnificent Disappointment* (Nampa, ID: Pacific Press Publishing Association, 1994), p. 5.
10. Letter, I. N. Pike to Bro. Smith, n.d., quoted in *RH*, April 23, 1857.

Organization and the Meetinghouse in Jamaica: 1860–1875

Instead of evolving into an organized denomination during the 1850s, Sabbatarianism remained a movement within the broader spectrum of Adventism. In this respect, seventh-day Sabbath keepers followed the precedent of Millerism, which had also been a movement, not a denomination. The Millerites' expulsion from their churches had also left them bitter and suspicious of organized religion.

However, in 1860, enough Sabbatarians overcame their bad memories and wary attitudes to decide to incorporate and adopt the name of Seventh-day Adventist, a tag that served two purposes. It disclosed that both the seventh-day Sabbath and the second advent formed the foundation of their beliefs, and it distinguished them from the more numerous varieties of Sunday-keeping Adventists classified under the loose-fitting rubric of first-day adventists.[1] Organization of the Seventh-day Adventist corporate body continued until 1863 as the new denomination formed conferences of churches, most often according to state boundaries, and finally a General Conference to oversee the entire structure.

Organization of the Jamaica Church

Records do not exist to tell later generations how large the denomination was in 1860, but estimates suggest about 3,000. Of that approximate total, a speculative guess would place about twenty in Jamaica, Vermont. Visiting ministers found the tiny flock burdened by spiritual shortcomings, but as shepherds of wandering sheep, they regarded the Jamaica Sabbath keepers as a spiritual challenge rather than a lost cause. In February 1860, C. W. Sperry returned, this time with D. T. Bourdeau, to preach and render pastoral help. The two ministers described the small group as "weighed down" and having "passed through much affliction,"[2] although they did not explain the problems. Two years later another minister, A. S. Hutchins, was more specific. He noted a lack of brotherliness and unity among the company of Sabbatarians, but most of them were resolved to "suffer with Jesus," he said. Summarizing his conversations with them, he wrote that "hearty confessions were made, and wrongs righted."[3]

Visiting ministers found the tiny flock burdened by spiritual shortcomings, but as shepherds of wandering sheep, they regarded the Jamaica Sabbath keepers as a spiritual challenge rather than a lost cause.

Months later, in the autumn of 1862, Hutchins organized a Seventh-day Adventist Church in Jamaica to satisfy a felt need for more order.[4] An undated record kept by an unknown member lists nine charter members from the Pike, Bourn, and Wilder families.[5] Because names of other Sabbatarian families living in Jamaica appeared in the *Review and Herald*, we are safe to conjecture that not all of the Sabbatarians joined the newly formed congregation.[6]

The Vermont Conference of Seventh-day Adventists also organized in 1862, but not until 1865 did the fledgling Jamaica church officially unite with the state organization.[7] Practically speaking, however, the Jamaica congregation functioned between 1862 and 1865 as though it were an official part of the conference. Ministers, including the conference president, kept Jamaica on their itineraries, and members in Jamaica contributed to conference finances through the traditional Seventh-day Adventist voluntary giving plan called Systematic Benevolence. Following this program, church members pledged specific amounts of money to the conference for a designated period, usually a year.[8]

If clergymen expressed concern about the spiritual problems confronting the members of the Jamaica church, they nevertheless had reasons for confidence. After visiting the congregation in 1863, Hutchins assured readers of the *Review* that the "plan of S. B. [Systematic Benevolence] is carried out. I never have seen any, more ready and earnest on the point than some here."[9]

Some questioned the financial competency of the newly formed denomination, headquartered in Battle Creek, Michigan. But Isaac Pike's son, C. N. Pike, a charter member in Jamaica, publicly proclaimed his loyalty to Adventism and his faith in the denomination by loaning it money, even against the advice of friends. He wanted the Adventist community to know that he had received the payoff of his loan before it expired. "So much for taking counsel of those who have no interest in the truth," he chortled.[10]

It was Sarah Nichols, however, who expressed the spiritual conviction that all Adventist pastors could wish for their spiritual sheep. In a twenty-line poem, "True Happiness," that expressed her continued faith in the second advent, she contrasted transient pleasures of this earth with her hope in a heavenly future. "This hope points us yonder for rest," she penned, "Where pleasures bloom not to decay, / Where the heart shall no more be opprest, / And sorrow shall vanish away."

However great was the need for Adventists in Jamaica to confess their mistakes, right their wrongs, and cultivate a sense of brotherliness, their faith in the old Millerite message of the return of Christ was alive and well. To encourage Adventist readers everywhere, James White published Sarah's poem on the front page of the *Review*.[11]

A. C. Bourdeau and the Jamaica Church

After becoming the third president of the Vermont Conference in 1865, A. C. Bourdeau—D. T. Bourdeau's older brother—assumed a more aggressive attitude toward the southern part of the state than previous ministers had shown.[12] It was not long before prospects among Seventh-day Adventists in Jamaica improved. The new president divided Vermont into four church districts. Three were in the north. Jamaica was in the fourth district that extended southward from the lower side of the Braintree township in central Vermont to include all of the southern half of the state. At a central location in each district, Bourdeau hoped to conduct quarterly gatherings for all churches and members.[13] In District 4, Jamaica became that gathering point. It was not a hard choice for Bourdeau to make. Jamaica was the only church in District 4.

During his six-week tour of southern Vermont in March and April 1867, Bourdeau discovered that the church in Jamaica had slipped to eight members, but that another half dozen Sabbath keepers from the town of Vernon had moved to the vicinity. He conducted six meetings, emphasizing Systematic Benevolence, and planted the idea that the congregation needed a permanent meetinghouse instead of gathering in private homes for worship.[14]

Although Bourdeau hoped to return to Jamaica before the end of the summer to spend several weeks in pastoral work, he was unable to fulfill his plan until February. From February 8 to 16, 1868, nine days in the dead of winter, including two weekends, he preached fourteen times, visited widely, and reclaimed backslidden believers.

Credit: Archives, Statistics, and Research, General Conference of Seventh-day Adventists

A.C. Bourdeau (1834–1916)

Bourdeau's work brought results. He baptized seven new members, and four others joined the congregation. "This church have become so numerous," he reported, "that they cannot easily hold their meetings in a private house." Although motivated to erect a church of their own, the members could not decide where to build. They lived in two concentrations, separated by about three miles, and until they could agree, their hope for a church building would have to wait.[15]

Bourdeau returned in June 1868. The congregation had decided to build the meetinghouse near Isaac Pike's home on the banks of the North Branch of Ball Mountain Brook and had collected lumber, but the members stalled on the question of financial support for their project. Bourdeau found them discouraged. He spent a week with them, renewing their commitments to Systematic Benevolence and rolling up his sleeves to work with them on church construction. Even with this demanding schedule, he still found time to conduct five meetings. With assistance before he left, he framed in the new meetinghouse, and when he left, the structure was nearly enclosed.[16]

Bourdeau's visit pumped fresh adrenalin into the congregation. Three-and-a-half months later at the annual session of the Vermont Conference, a motion reached the floor to allow the congregation in Jamaica to retain "half of their S. B. funds, and more if the Executive Committee so direct, to aid in finishing their house of worship." The conference secretary did not indicate whether the motion carried or failed, but circumstances favored Jamaica. The following year delegates to the conference session approved an identical motion to benefit the church at East Richford.[17]

During the year from 1867 to 1868, the Jamaica church had added about twenty-five members. While visiting the congregation in June 1868, Bourdeau inspired thirty-three members, some of them probably new, to pledge $122.20 in Systematic Benevolence to the conference funds. These donors represented nearly 13 percent of the Vermont Conference membership of 256. However, the money from Jamaica amounted to only 7 percent of the total from all members in Vermont for the year.

These figures reveal that pledges from the Jamaica church were below average, which corroborated an assessment Hutchins later made when he concluded that the congregation was financially weak. In effect, the proposal to permit the Jamaica church to retain half of its pledges was a request for the conference to relinquish about 3.5 percent of its revenue.[18] The Vermont Conference was already operating on a proverbial shoestring, and it was evident that a concession of this size would drain a significant amount from the conference coffers.

In November 1868, only a month after the conference session, Bourdeau went back to Jamaica to encourage the congregation. He found everyone mourning the death of the only son of Emery and Martha Sage, members living near the unfinished meetinghouse. Sensitive to the sadness and gloom pervading the church, the conference president did not hold many meetings but spent three weeks going from home to home to heal broken spirits.[19]

In June 1870, Nahum Orcutt, the conference secretary, spent three weekends in Jamaica. He was impressed with the "neat, convenient house of worship" that the congregation hoped to dedicate within weeks. He preached ten times and visited the homes of members, but he could not restrain his concern for the spiritual well-being of the members. They should "expect better days" if they "keep very near the Lord," he reported.[20]

Two months after Orcutt's visit, a shakeup in conference leadership directly affected the Jamaica church. After five years as president of the conference, Bourdeau stepped down. Orcutt, who had been the conference secretary for only two years, also left office.[21] Both men returned to full-time pastoring. Whether planned or not, Orcutt's visit to Jamaica had opened the door to a new assignment. Announcing in March 1871, that his "P. O. address is Jamaica, Vt.," he moved to the community to become what Warren E. Booker calls the "first settled pastor" of the church.[22]

Nahum Orcutt's Pastorate in Southern Vermont

Orcutt was a relatively new Seventh-day Adventist. Leading up to 1864, he was a farmer in Troy, Vermont, who scoffed at religion, but his reading of a study about the seventh-day Sabbath brought abrupt changes to his life. He and his wife began to observe Saturday instead of Sunday. Three years later in 1867, they sold their farm and moved briefly to the newly established Seventh-day Adventist health institute at Battle Creek, Michigan. There, Nahum hoped to recover the health that he had ruined by "filthy habits." We can assume that his improvement was rapid. Only months later in early 1868, he and his wife were back in Vermont.

At this time Orcutt was about forty-five years old. He was not reticent, and his often-expressed faith captured the attention of Seventh-day Adventist ministers in Vermont. Recognizing him as self-taught but a potential candidate for full-time ministry, they were quick to yield church pulpits to him. He accompanied A. C. Bourdeau to Jamaica in February 1868, and conducted a memorial service for an infant daughter of C. N. and Emeline Pike five months after her death, a delay caused by the fact that this was probably the first visit by a minister after she had died. In October 1868, delegates to the Vermont Conference elected Orcutt secretary of their conference. He was a licensed minister, but in 1869 he was ordained.[23]

In April 1871, less than a month-and-a-half after Orcutt's move to southern Vermont, Bourdeau also traveled to Jamaica, where he had invested so much emotional and physical energy. He reported that the new meetinghouse was complete. The construction had demanded hard work, sacrifice, and perseverance. An anonymous recorder of the event recalled that the contributions, some of which probably occurred after the congregation occupied the new sanctuary, had required the time and effort of many. Abraham Bourn had donated the land. William White paid for the stove and the pipes. William's son, Cassius, helped to make the seats and arranged for the purchase of an organ. Another of William's sons, Flavius, laid the floor of the platform with three-inch squares of dark and light wood. Francis Richmond fashioned the pulpit. The seating capacity was about 200.[24]

"By the blessing of God," Bourdeau wrote, "they now have a respectable meetinghouse, all paid for without receiving any assistance from abroad." Although the sanctuary itself was ready in 1871, members were still building sheds "to shelter their teams when they go to meeting."[25]

Doubtless, the Jamaica church members felt twice blessed with a pastor to accompany their new meetinghouse. But Orcutt was more than the settled pastor of the Jamaica church. He became a regional pastor to shepherd other Seventh-day Adventist families scattered in southern Vermont and to evangelize as he could find time, an assignment he assumed with zeal. His appointment as a regional pastor was typical Seventh-day Adventist practice. Rarely in the nineteenth century did any church enjoy a resident pastor. Instead, ministers traveled from congregation to congregation.

Rarely in the nineteenth century did any church enjoy a resident pastor. Instead, ministers traveled from congregation to congregation.

In July 1871, Orcutt reported that since his arrival he had spent "every Sabbath but one with the church here," which meant that he recognized his duties in Jamaica, but he had also preached ten times to "friends from the outside." Among the friends from the outside were a Methodist church in Bondville and a Baptist church in South Londonderry, communities within a ten-mile radius of Jamaica. He also visited Seventh-day Adventist families in Andover, about twenty miles north of Jamaica. He assured Adventist leaders that his torrid pace was not harming him. Both he and his wife were enjoying "more than usual health" after their illness the previous autumn.[26]

More than three months later, in mid-October, Orcutt's report recounted his attendance at the conference camp meeting. Following this event, he visited several churches in northern Vermont. Returning to his assigned district, he devoted a weekend to the small company in Andover, baptizing three and admitting four to church membership. The number of official members in Andover rose to eleven. What remained of his time since his last report he had "spent with the church in Jamaica."[27]

Orcutt's diligence bore results. During A. C. Bourdeau's travels around Vermont with Lewis Bean, the conference president, in December 1872, and January 1873, he noted that the Jamaica church was the second-largest in the Vermont Conference. While he found satisfaction in this statistic, he admitted to trouble in Jamaica. Some members were taking positions contrary to fundamental teachings of the denomination, but he did not explain what they were. Divisive attitudes were splitting the congregation. Bourdeau and Bean labored hard to mend the weakened church. The seven meetings they conducted were their "most important" gatherings, they said.[28]

By the end of 1873, the era of A. C. Bourdeau and Nahum Orcutt in Jamaica ended. Approximately ten years younger than Orcutt but with a stronger presence and more experience, Bourdeau was more influential. He became the president of the Tract and Missionary Society of the Vermont Conference, an arm of the denomination that promoted literature distribution and other outreach activities. He later worked in many different fields, some of them in Canada and Europe. Orcutt transferred to New Jersey, followed by assignments in Massachusetts and Florida.[29]

For Seventh-day Adventists in Jamaica, Bourdeau and Orcutt had been the dominant ministerial figures in their experience since the formal organization of the denomination. Although Lewis Bean, the Vermont Conference president beginning in 1870, traveled to southern Vermont as he made his rounds among the churches, in comparison to Bourdeau he gave scant attention to Jamaica. The first decade-and-a-half of denominational organization was a period of uncertainty for the Jamaica congregation, but the meetinghouse stood as a monument to Bourdeau's vision for this remote community.

Notes

1. Detailed reports of the first organizational meetings were front-page news in three successive editions of the *Advent Review and Sabbath Herald*, October 9, 16, and 23, 1860.
2. "Meetings in New England," *RH*, February 16, 1860. Sperry was a Sabbatarian minister who visited Jamaica in 1856. See note 12 of this chapter for biographical information about D. T. Bourdeau.
3. "Meetings in N. H. and Southern Vt.," *RH*, March 4, 1862. Hutchins had been a Free Will Baptist minister who joined the Sabbatarians in 1852.
4. "Report of Meetings," *RH*, November 18, 1862.
5. "History of the Pikes Falls Church," no author, n.d. This is a single-page record that Flavius White, a member of the White family, members of Jamaica Seventh-day Adventist Church beginning in 1869, gave to his niece. It is regarded as an accurate statement of the beginnings of the Jamaica church. No one signed the paper, but Elizabeth Hurd Greene, whose family were members of the Jamaica church until the late 1930s, believes that an unidentified member of the Pike family prepared the statement. Hereafter this source is cited by its complete title.
6. Two other family names appearing in the 1863 issues of the *RH* are Johnson and Barr. See issues of March 3 and December 29, 1863.
7. "Northern New England Conference," *SDA Encyclopedia*, 2nd rev. ed., vol. M–Z, p. 351. "Fourth Annual Session of the Vermont State Conference," *RH*, July 11, 1865.
8. See travel schedules for ministers in *RH*, June 14, 1863; December 20, 1864. Note contributions by the Jamaica church to the Vermont Conference fund in *RH*, May 26, 1863; December 15, 1863.
9. "Meetings in Vermont," *RH*, December 8, 1863.
10. "That Money," *RH*, April 15, 1862.
11. "True Happiness," *RH*, September 25, 1866.
12. A. C. Bourdeau and his younger brother, D. T. Bourdeau, were members of a French-Canadian family who settled near Enosburgh, Vermont, in 1835. The community around their original home is now known as Bordoville. The Bourdeau family converted to Protestantism in 1840. Beginning in 1851 the teenaged brothers, A. C. and D. T., attended the Grand Ligne Mission Institute in Canada and later became active workers among Baptists in both Canada and Vermont. By 1860 the two brothers and most of the family had become Sabbatarian Adventists. A. C. and D. T. served as prominent Seventh-day

Adventist ministers until their deaths in 1916 and 1905, respectively. "Seventh-day Adventists, a Letter from Rev. A. C. Bourdeau in *VHG*, vol. 2, pp. 147, 148; "Bourdeau, Augustin Cornelius" and "Bourdeau, Daniel T," *SDA Encyclopedia,* 2nd rev. ed., vol. A–L, pp. 224, 225.

13. "Arrangements for Meetings in Vermont and Canada East," *RH*, November 26, 1867.
14. "The Cause in Vermont," *RH*, July 30, 1867.
15. "Labors in Southern Vermont," *RH*, March 3, 1868.
16. "Report from Bro. A. C. Bourdeau," *RH*, August 18, 1868.
17. "Sixth Annual Session of the Vermont State Conference," *RH*, October 20, 1868; "Vermont State Conference," *RH*, November 2, 1869.
18. I have adapted these statistics from the report of the Vermont Conference, "Sixth Annual Session of the Vermont State Conference," *RH*, October 20, 1868.
19. "The Cause in Jamaica, Vt.," *RH*, November 17, 1868; "Report from Bro. A. C. Bourdeau," *RH*, December 1, 1868.
20. "Report of Labor," *RH*, August 2, 1870.
21. "Vermont State Conference," *RH*, September 13, 1870.
22. Booker, *Historical Notes*, p. 41. Booker incorrectly lists Orcutt's pastorate beginning in 1884.
23. I have summarized this paragraph from numerous reports in *RH*: "Both Sides," November 29, 1864; "Sabbath, or No Sabbath?" January 3, 1865; "The Lord Hath Wrought," August 1, 1865; "Meetings in Vermont," April 9, 1867; "Notes from D. T. Bourdeau," February 4, 1868; "Labors in Southern Vermont," March 3, 1868; "Obituary Notices," March 10, 1868; "Report from Bro. A. C. Bourdeau," September 18, 1868; "Sixth Annual Session of the Vermont State Conference," October 20, 1868; "Vermont State Conference," November 2, 1869.
24. "History of the Pikes Falls Church."
25. "Vermont," *RH*, May 23, 1871.
26. "Report of Labors," *RH*, August 15, 1871.
27. "Vermont," *RH*, October 24, 1871.
28. "Vermont," *RH*, January 28, 1873.
29. See biographical sketch of A. C. Bourdeau in *SDA Encyclopedia*, 2nd rev. ed., vol. A–L, p. 224. Orcutt's career is traceable in his scattered reports to the *Review and Herald* until his death in 1897.

A New Beginning with A. S. Hutchins: 1875–1885

Lewis Bean's five-year presidency of the Vermont Conference ended in 1875. Delegates to the annual business session of the conference that year elected A. S. Hutchins as his successor. A former Free Will Baptist minister, the new president was no stranger to Jamaica.[1] Not only had he visited the church several times in the 1860s but he also had organized the church in 1862. However, for more than a decade while he labored in many parts of the state, others had assumed leadership roles in southern Vermont.

A. S. Hutchins's Patriarchal Reputation

Adventists in Vermont were well aware of Hutchins's pastoral style that was more patriarchal than hard driving. During his stopover among the sometimes-problematic members in Jamaica in February 1876, he visited nearly every family, conducted meetings for three days, and officiated at a communion service. He left hearts filled with "hope and courage," he penned.

Hutchins's report of his visit left little room to doubt his understanding and accommodating attitude. "We cannot expect the amount of missionary labor that we do in some other localities," he reflected paternalistically about the Jamaica church, observing that the members were scattered in the "thinly settled Green Mountains." They lived far from markets, they were financially strapped, but they only asked for time to fulfill their pledges to Systematic Benevolence, a favor that Hutchins seemed more than ready to grant. In spite of his fatherly understanding of circumstances in Jamaica, Hutchins admitted that the spiritual strength of the congregation had not increased "proportionately with its numbers."[2]

Repeatedly, Hutchins had commended the Jamaica members for their loyalty to the plan of Systematic Benevolence in spite of their economically weak circumstances. When seeking financial commitment to the denomination, he was more prone to offer a carrot rather than a rhetorical whip disguised as a biblical reprimand. His understanding of the congregation paid off. Members fulfilled their pledges to Systematic Benevolence and made special donations as well. In 1876, ten members who represented nine families of the Jamaica church pledged and paid $300 to support the denomination's new college in Battle Creek, Michigan.[3]

Empathy for the Jamaica congregation because of its financially weak potential was

Credit: Archives, Statistics, and Research, General Conference of Seventh-day Adventists

A.S. Hutchins (1823–1894)

characteristic of how Hutchins dealt with issues. But the location of the church on the southern periphery of the Seventh-day Adventist community in Vermont produced problems that remained beyond his healing touch. This circumstance had plagued the group since the Great Disappointment in 1844. After that demoralizing event, Millerites in Jamaica waited nearly eight years until a minister arrived with encouragement.

The attention that Bourdeau and Orcutt gave to Jamaica could not erase the fact that the strength of Seventh-day Adventists in Vermont lay in the northern half of the state. When the Vermont Conference convened its annual camp meeting in the northern community of Essex Junction in August 1875, attendees from twenty-four Vermont communities pitched their tents, of which seventeen were located north of Montpelier, or the upper 40 percent of the state. Of those seventeen towns, eleven were in the northwestern corner of the state and six in the northeastern corner. Believers from only seven towns south of Montpelier attended the camp. Jamaica was the only community represented in the entire southern half of Vermont. Additionally, two groups attended from Canada, both coming from towns less than forty miles from the Vermont line.[4]

It is probable that there were Adventist communities whose members did not attend the camp meeting, but the attendance at the 1875 gathering confirmed that the overwhelming weight of membership was in northern Vermont, particularly the northwest corner. A buffer of about seventy miles isolated the Adventist meetinghouse in Jamaica from the nearest Seventh-day Adventist community in the Brookfield–Roxbury vicinity in the center of the state. Other than those in Jamaica, only a few scattered members dotted the southern half of the state.

All of this meant that maintaining Jamaica as an effective part of the Vermont Conference was more expensive than the costs connected to a congregation in the north. While Vermont Conference leaders visited Jamaica, the long distance they had to travel to southern Vermont made their trips more costly in both money and time as compared to their visits to churches in the northern part of the state. It was clear that only by concerted effort could the Jamaica church maintain its connection with the rest of the state's members.

Isaac Sanborn and Membership Growth

Hutchins, however, regularly toured the entire state, spreading his influence with patriarchal gentility. With specific evangelistic plans in mind, he organized two tent companies in 1878 and invited a well-known Adventist minister, Isaac Sanborn from Wisconsin, to conduct back-to-back summer meetings in southern Vermont. The first would take place in Weston, about twenty miles from Jamaica, and the next in West Townshend, only five miles from the village of Jamaica. Sanborn planned to launch his campaigns with a revival in the Jamaica church. In June, Hutchins traveled south to welcome the evangelist, who did not disappoint the conference president. His inspirational meetings, spread over two weekends and punctuated by the baptism of seven new members, energized the congregation.[5]

The support that the Jamaica church gave to Sanborn's evangelistic plans was impressive. One member furnished an organ that added much to the meetings in Weston, and a large number from the Jamaica church swelled his tent audiences in West Townshend. Attendance fluctuated as high as 200.[6]

Sanborn had not come to Jamaica as a permanent pastor but rather as an evangelist-on-loan before he moved on to Virginia. He remained only briefly in Vermont, leaving in December 1878, but while there, he pastored the Jamaica church and nurtured the new converts from his tent meetings. Meanwhile, he continued with evangelism in Rawsonville and South Londonderry. He preached his final sermon in Jamaica on the weekend of December 21.

"It was indeed gratifying to hear the testimonies and prayers of several brethren and sisters who have embraced the Sabbath under the labors of Bro. Sanborn," wrote Hutchins, who had traveled to Jamaica for the evangelist's last appearance. No reports show how many new members the guest preacher had gained during his six-month evangelistic campaign, but in October he baptized five in Weston and added twelve to the Jamaica church.[7]

Although he was not an assigned pastor of southern Vermont, Sanborn fulfilled the duties of pastor more effectively than any other person since Nahum Orcutt. Among the Jamaica members, he kindled a spiritual fire and a yearning for a permanent pastor. Only weeks after he left Vermont, church members requested Hutchins to supply pastoral help to continue the work that Sanborn had begun. Hutchins found a ready candidate in R. S. Owen, a young, newly credentialed minister fresh from the altar of ordination. The new pastor assumed his duties in the spring of 1879. By mid-June he conducted a set of meetings in Jamaica and reported that church members would encourage new converts in weekly gatherings.[8]

But Owen did not remain long. Within two years he transferred to northern Vermont, which left the Jamaica church where it had been for years—on the sidelines. As conference president, Hutchins was responsible for Owen's switch to other fields, and he had little choice but to resume his own circuit-riding pastoral role in Jamaica.

As much as the Jamaica members wanted a permanent pastor, they had to acknowledge that the Vermont Conference did not have enough ministers to go around and that the conference did not assign pastors exclusively to a single church. In 1881, seven ministers—five ordained and two holding only ministerial licenses—shared the responsibility of pastoring the fourteen organized churches in Vermont. Among the seven were the officers of the Vermont Conference.[9] All of them lived in the northern half of the state.

Arguably, to assign a permanent pastor to southern Vermont, which, in practical terms meant Jamaica, would have given the lone church in the south preferential treatment.

Because congregations in that region were relatively close together, they did not have to wait as long as members in Jamaica waited between clerical visits. Arguably, to assign a permanent pastor to southern Vermont, which, in practical terms meant Jamaica, would have given the lone church in the south preferential treatment.

Contributing to the concentration of pastors in the northern half of the state was the fact that Canadian believers in the Eastern Townships were also under the supervision of Vermont ministers. Their reports to the *Review* indicated that they frequently crossed the border into Canada. Denis Fortin has explained that even after the Quebec Conference organized in 1880, Vermont pastors continued to extend their influence in Quebec's Eastern Townships.[10] As for the members of the Jamaica church, knowing the facts of the situation helped, but it was small compensation for the neglect they felt.

In the summer of 1881 Hutchins again traveled to Jamaica, "more than twenty-five years . . . since my first visit," he remembered nostalgically. Some from that early group of leftover Millerites were still members of the congregation. Like other conference leaders before him, Hutchins detected lax church discipline. But most encouraging to him was the fact that the church now claimed about sixty members, although some were "hopelessly backslidden." Hutchins reacted in his typical fashion, more conciliatory than condemnatory. His meetings on three successive Sabbaths and during the intervening weekdays, combined with house-to-house visits, brought confessions and recommitment from many.

Hutchins conceded that "flying visits" by him or any other minister were not the answer to the problems of the Jamaica church. His fellow conference leaders agreed that southern Vermont needed a pastor to oversee the Jamaica church and to expand its activities in the region. But they also knew that before the conference could justify the expense of assigning a regional minister to Jamaica, southern Vermont needed more members and more organized congregations.

Already Hutchins was preparing the way for that additional pastoral presence in southern Vermont. Immediately before arriving in Jamaica in 1881, he had organized a church that combined the families of Andover and Weston into a single congregation,[11] which meant that two churches, rather than one, in the region now needed pastoral care. Weeks later at the 1881 camp meeting, Jamaica church members took advantage of this need by submitting a formal request to the conference for a pastor. Convening for this annual conference business session in August, delegates chose to deny the request without actually voting to reject it. They dodged the question by leaving the decision up to the conference committee,[12] where little if any hope existed for the petition from Jamaica.

But the realization that inconsistent pastoral oversight for the Jamaica church produced ups and downs in the spiritual journeys of too many members continued to nag conference leaders. Recovering the wanderers had become an uncomfortable but necessary commonplace. Probably all of this was weighing on Hutchins's mind when he asked G. W. Page, a licensed minister with experience in evangelism, to help him organize a two-week revival in Jamaica beginning in December 1882.

Without any hope of establishing a permanent pastor, Hutchins and Page timed their visit to coincide with the installation of local church leaders for the ensuing year. The two ministers used the occasion to motivate members to reach out to the public for more conversions. They also encouraged literature distribution and resurrected the defunct temperance society, an activity that R. S. Owen had initiated to promote healthful living among both church members and the Jamaica locals.[13]

Denominational Leaders Visit the Jamaica Church

The December revival was only the beginning of Hutchins's ideas about how to strengthen the Jamaica congregation. In 1883, when George I. Butler, president of the General Conference of Seventh-day Adventists, toured Vermont, Hutchins saw to it that his itinerary began in Jamaica.[14] Butler was a Vermonter with relatively distinguished lineage who was returning home. As the grandson of Baptist preacher Ezra Pitt Butler who had also been governor of Vermont from 1826 to 1828, George I. grew up in Waterbury where the family owned a starch factory. His father had listened to the Millerite message and, along with his family, had joined the movement. They were among the disappointed on October 22, 1844.[15]

At the time of Butler's visit to Vermont in 1883, Seventh-day Adventist total membership exceeded 17,000 and had spread to Europe. Of this number, fewer than 400 lived in Vermont. The Vermont Conference ranked fourteenth in membership on a list of twenty-four conferences in the United States and Canada.[16] Butler had attended the business sessions of the Vermont Conference in 1881 and 1882, but this trip took him to the local churches. He intended his visit be an inspiration as he rubbed shoulders with members. The importance of his tour beginning in Jamaica may have been symbolic, but it was nonetheless important to the local church. It was in this too-often overlooked corner of Vermont that the denominational president would derive his first impression of the conference during his three-week visit.

When Butler reached Jamaica on April 7, the Green Mountain winter was barely yielding to spring thaws. He commented that if "we had not been favored by good weather just at the right time, we should not have been able to reach the place of meeting." Members from a neighboring church, in all likelihood the Andover-Weston congregation, also attended. Butler was pleased with what he saw in Jamaica. "The Lord's blessing was present," he said, "if we could judge by the excellent attention and the moistened eye." Yet he detected what other visiting ministers had also often seen in the Jamaica church: some members suffered "great affliction," a pastoral phrase that meant some were not coping well with spiritual challenges to their faith.[17]

Although Hutchins could not often bring in denominational leaders to inspire his churches nor assure all churches in the Vermont Conference that an ordained minister would officiate at their quarterly meetings, he made certain that he paid a pastoral visit to Jamaica whenever possible. In July, three months after Butler's appearance, Hutchins journeyed again to Jamaica, "no providence preventing," he said, to conduct a communion service. The visit also allowed him to encourage the members of the congregation who had established a branch Sabbath school—Bible classes on Saturday—in Windham.[18]

In March 1884, Hutchins scheduled S. N. Haskell, another denominational stalwart, to visit Jamaica. Haskell was president of three conferences at the same time, the organizer of the denominational Tract and

Missionary Society, and the leading founder of South Lancaster Academy in Massachusetts, where he lived and spent much of his time.[19] His reputation as a promoter of education was well-known.

Hutchins was on hand for Haskell's visit. Although Haskell put in a busy weekend at the church, he was accustomed to crowded agendas. He promoted literature distribution, a project close to his heart, and with Hutchins's support, broached the idea that the Jamaica church should establish a school for children in the congregation.[20]

Seventh-day Adventist education had officially begun in 1872 in Michigan, but it was primarily a program for young adults, not elementary schools for children. At that time, denominational leaders did not encourage congregations to establish a church-operated equivalent to a common school. Only a few courageous souls had bucked this trend and inspired churches to add an elementary school to their activities. Haskell was one of those who bucked the trend, but despite his stature in the denomination, his disagreement with the prevailing attitude in Adventist officialdom had not yet ignited a movement. After founding South Lancaster Academy in 1882, he began promoting the new school as a place for young Seventh-day Adventist adults to prepare for careers in teaching, which in his mind meant teaching in Adventist schools. Notwithstanding his enthusiasm, it was not until nearly the turn of the century that his ideas caught on. Meanwhile, he satisfied himself with such visits as he made to Jamaica.

The reaction in Jamaica was immediate. Nellie Richmond, a member of the congregation, wrote that some "very interesting remarks were made by Bro. Haskell regarding the school enterprise." Haskell convinced Nellie and her peers in Jamaica that they needed at least a summer school where their "children and others could be instructed in missionary work." Before Haskell left, the Jamaica church appointed a committee of three to plan for the school and "carry it into effect."[21]

Hutchins was solidly behind the plan. He helped to lead the discussions and nudged the church forward to accomplish the project. Two months later, he was back in Jamaica, not only to help a visiting evangelist conduct a revival but also to support the church's decision about the school. "It is high time for our people to awake to the dangers which threaten our children," he warned, implying that Adventist children of school age should attend a school where instruction in Adventism was a recognized part of the program. Hutchins let it be known that he was pleased that the church had requested South Lancaster Academy to furnish "a competent teacher" for the proposed school. He also remarked that the entire Vermont Conference would be watching the goings-on in Jamaica.[22]

Before the month was over, Laura Bee began classes in the Jamaica church. Hutchins could not let the occasion pass without pointing out that Jamaica was leading the way in Vermont. No one could doubt his agreement with what was happening in both South Lancaster and Jamaica. "Education is far more valuable than gold," he declared. "Who can value a Bible education?"[23]

Hutchins understated the case when he said that the entire conference would be watching. In recognition of the solemn nature of the two leading issues facing delegates to the forthcoming camp meeting in Burlington, he announced a period of fasting and prayer. Besides public evangelism, the question of education was on the agenda. Significantly, one of the founders of the Seventh-day Adventist Church, fifty-seven-year-old Ellen White, was to be present for the camp meeting. A dozen years earlier in 1872, she had also laid the philosophical platform for Seventh-day Adventist education with a thirty-page essay, "Proper Education."[24]

The delegates did not wait long for a chance to show where they stood on the matter. On the morning of the fifth day of business, a resolution to encourage all churches in the conference to establish schools "like the one at Jamaica" reached the floor. Without acting, the delegates adjourned the meeting but continued their discussion in the afternoon. A candid assessment of the problems connected to church-sponsored elementary schools followed, but the resolution carried. Given the paucity of church school teachers, a second resolution the next day called for the Vermont Conference to offer financial support to prospective students from the state who enrolled for teacher-preparation training at South Lancaster Academy.[25] That fall, thirteen took advantage of the offer.[26] Hutchins could hardly have done more to give the Jamaica church a more prominent place on the Adventist map.

Before the next Vermont camp meeting and conference session, Hutchins trekked once again to Jamaica, helping to arrange for M. Augusta Green to replace Laura Bee as the teacher of the church school. The first school had been a summer session, but the new plan called for a twelve-week schedule, beginning in September.[27]

Suffering from declining health and advancing age (he was sixty-two years old), Hutchins left the presidency of the Vermont Conference in 1885. While visiting the Jamaica church the previous year, Haskell had observed that Hutchins's physical constitution was weakening.[28] The delegates to the 1885 conference session voted their "sincere appreciation for his faithful, conscientious, and effectual service."[29]

For nine more years, Hutchins remained active, but his roles were always less conspicuous than conference president. Many congregations knew him as a friend and spiritual mentor, but few had felt his warm, understanding leadership more than the members in Jamaica. Much as a result of his efforts, by 1885, the Jamaica church had become a pillar of strength in the Vermont Conference.

Notes

1. For a brief sketch of Hutchins's life, see *RH*, July 17, 1894.
2. "Vermont," *RH*, March 23, 1876.
3. "College Pledges," *RH*, October 26, 1876.
4. "The Seventh-day Adventist Camp-Meeting," *RH*, September 2, 1875.
5. "Jamaica, Vermont," *RH*, June 20, 1878.
6. See Sanborn's reports in *RH*, "Vermont, Tent No. 1, Weston," July 25, 1878; "Vermont, Tent No. 1, West Townshend, August 12," August 22, 1878; "Vermont, Tent No. 1, West Townshend," September 5, 1878.
7. "Vermont," *RH*, October 24, 1878; "Vermont," *RH*, January 16, 1879.
8. "Calling for Help," *RH*, March 20, 1879; "Vermont," *RH*, June 26, 1879.
9. "Vermont Conference," *RH*, October 11, 1881.
10. Denis Fortin, *Adventism in Quebec* (Berrien Springs, MI: Andrews University Press, 2004), pp. 91–136.
11. "Vermont," *RH*, June 19, 1881.
12. "Vermont Conference," *RH*, October 11, 1881.
13. "Vermont," *RH*, January 16, 1883.
14. "To the Brethren in Vermont," *RH*, March 13, 1883; "Appointments," *RH*, March 27, 1883.
15. Emmet K. Vande Vere, *Rugged Heart, the Story of George I. Butler* (Nashville, TN: Southern Publishing Association, 1979), pp. 9–13.
16. *Seventh-day Adventist Yearbook*, 1884, p. 73. The *Yearbook* is the annual denominational directory published by the General Conference. Hereafter this source cited as *Yearbook*.
17. "Labor in Vermont," *RH*, May 15, 1883.
18. "Quarterly Meetings," *RH*, June 19, 1883; "Vermont," *RH*, August 7, 1883.
19. For a short outline of Haskell's activities, see "Haskell, Stephen Nelson," *SDA Encyclopedia*, 2nd rev. ed., vol. A–L, pp. 669, 670; "South Lancaster Academy," ibid., vol. M–Z, pp. 651, 652.
20. "The Cause in New England," *RH*, March 25, 1884.

21. "Our Meeting in Vermont," *RH*, April 1, 1884.
22. "Vermont," *RH*, June 10, 1884.
23. "The Jamaica Church School," ibid.
24. Ellen G. White, *Testimonies for the Church*, vol. 3 (Mountain View, CA: Pacific Press Publishing Association, 1948), pp. 131–160. The first printing of this essay occurred in 1872. See Arthur L. White, *Ellen G. White: The Progressive Years 1862–1876* (Hagerstown, MD: Review and Herald Publishing Association, 2002), pp. 342, 343.
25. "Vermont Conference Report," *RH*, October 7, 1884.
26. "Vermont," *RH*, November 25, 1884.
27. "The Cause in New England," *RH*, March 25, 1884.
28. "Vermont," *RH*, July 21, 1885.
29. "Vermont Conference Proceedings," *RH*, October 6, 1885.

Coming of Age: 1885–1895

By the time Hutchins left the conference presidency in 1885, the Jamaica church membership had risen to eighty-one.[1] Measured by Seventh-day Adventist standards in Vermont, as well as in all of New England, the Jamaica church was large. This distinction was noteworthy because Jamaica was a rural community. Ironically, the location of the church on the periphery of the conference, once deemed as an obstacle to its success, was about to become the congregation's best opportunity for progress.

Seven years before Hutchins retired from the presidency, Isaac Sanborn showed that the Jamaica church could be a base of operations for missionary outreach to much of southern Vermont. He preached in Weston, West Townshend, Rawsonville, and South Londonderry, but he relied on Jamaica as his headquarters and for support. R. S. Owen also made similar attempts, but on a lesser scale. However, no one capitalized on the idea successfully until I. E. Kimball took up work in the southern part of the state in 1885.

I. E. Kimball's Ministry

A promising pastoral recruit from Kansas, Kimball moved to the Vermont Conference in 1884.[2] Except for the Jamaica church and the small Andover-Weston congregation, both in the county's northwest quadrant, Windham County was nearly void of Seventh-day Adventists. Kimball visualized southern Vermont as a mission field with the Jamaica church as a source of personnel and the hub from which much of the outreach would emanate. As he saw circumstances, what had once been the primary drawback for the Jamaica church became an opportunity to create that critical mass of membership that Hutchins had required before assigning a permanent pastor to the region.

> *Kimball visualized southern Vermont as a mission field with the Jamaica church as a source of personnel and the hub from which much of the outreach would emanate.*

After performing pastoral duties in northern Vermont in late 1884, Kimball spent three days with the Jamaica church in January 1885, preaching four times before rushing farther south to Brattleboro. The reason for his haste was a decision to establish a mission in the largest population center in southeastern Vermont.

"Bro. Clayton and his wife from Jamaica are here now to engage in canvassing [selling religious literature]," Kimball wrote to the *Review* on January 21, adding that Brattleboro was his new address.[3] For Kimball and Clayton, the city and its environs were an open market for literature sales. Together, they worked through the community, selling books and papers.

Kimball made sure that his enthusiasm rubbed off on the members in Jamaica. Although he was not their resident pastor, in March he went back to preach to them, "one of the strongest churches of the state," he said. Unlike many other visiting speakers who observed a lack of spiritual commitment among the congregation, Kimball saw "unity and a very manifest zeal" to engage in the "cause," a term he applied to literature sales. Thirteen members of the Jamaica church signed up to become salespersons.[4]

Kimball's impact on the entire Vermont Conference was electric. His recent arrival in the state did not slow his rapid advancement. He had barely arrived in Vermont in 1884 before unusual circumstances catapulted him into leadership roles. Because the conference secretary was absent from the annual conference business session, Kimball performed the duties *pro tem*, only to find himself elected to that office before the session ended. When the conference delegates convened in mid-August the next year, they chose him to replace Hutchins as president.[5]

The contrast between the two men could hardly have been greater. Kimball was youthful and inexperienced. Only twenty-four years old, he had not yet reached his first birthday when Hutchins, who had been preaching since 1846,[6] organized the Jamaica church in 1862. Kimball did not become an ordained minister until the 1885 conference session. By the time that conference business session began, not only the members in Jamaica, but also the entire conference, knew this outgoing and aggressive young man.

No longer personally able to pursue his mission in Brattleboro because he was the new conference president, Kimball sent two other men to continue literature sales. In February 1886, he led a five-day revival in Jamaica, where he said the Spirit caused "an apparent stir in the camp." The church ordered seventy-five subscriptions to the *Signs of the Times*, the denominational missionary journal published weekly in California. Members agreed to send the papers to persons whose addresses they secured from the directory for Windham County. They would follow up with personal visits to discuss spiritual and religious issues.[7] Six months later at the annual meeting of the Vermont Conference Tract and Missionary Society, leaders in the individual churches recommended that all congregations in the state should adopt the plan that the Jamaica church had implemented.[8]

Because of its experimentation in education and missionary outreach, by the mid-1880s, the Jamaica church became a leader among the churches of the Vermont Conference. But southern Vermont remained without pastoral leadership, which meant that visits by ordained or sometimes licensed ministers were still the norm. Between 1885 and 1888, M. E. Kellogg, H. F. Barton, H. Peebles, C. L. Kellogg, T. H. Purdon, and H. W. Pierce conducted periodic revivals or preached in Jamaica on the few weekends they could spare, always assuring church leaders that the congregation was inspired and blessed.[9] As for Kimball himself, in less than two years, his energetic leadership propelled him into a new job: heading an evangelistic mission to Halifax, Nova Scotia. Before leaving Vermont, he toured the conference again, ending with a visit to southern Vermont and the Jamaica church.[10]

Kimball's work in Jamaica and southern Vermont reflected the emphasis that the denomination placed on literature sales. Adventist presses in Michigan and California published inspirational books and papers by the ton. Compelled by their conviction that literature distribution supplemented pastoral work, church leaders encouraged many members to commit to this work and went to great lengths to prepare them as salespersons. The goal was to inspire public reading about spiritual issues. Door-to-door book peddlers, most often called colporteurs but sometimes canvassers or agents, took orders for books they would deliver at a later date. Kimball's project in Brattleboro depended on the Jamaica church for colporteurs.

Near the end of the 1880s, conference officers named P. F. Bicknell as state agent, or supervisor of colporteurs in Vermont. Recognizing that the Jamaica church was already a source of these salespersons, he conducted a ten-day "drill" in the Jamaica church during October 1889, to prepare prospective colporteurs. Praying that "this large church may go forward," he also baptized eight in the chilled autumn waters of the creek that flowed near the church, four of whom became colporteurs.[11] The Jamaica church was flourishing.

Credit: Photo by the author

The North Branch Ball Mountain Brook that flowed only a few yards from the Adventist meetinghouse in Pikes Falls added to the rural setting of the church. In October 1889, P. F. Bicknell baptized eight in this stream, and in January 1893, William Covert postponed a baptism because the ice was too thick to break open.

After his short mission to Nova Scotia ended, Kimball returned to Vermont and eventually settled in Jamaica, in March 1892, to become the resident pastor in southern Vermont,[12] an event that the congregation had long awaited. He soon formed an evangelistic team that conducted meetings in Sunderland, about fifteen miles west of the Jamaica church in Bennington County.[13]

Kimball characterized Sunderland as spiritually lax, an oblique reference to the possibility that Ethan Allen's century-old deist movement in this region surrounding Bennington may have long since become less aggressive, but it was far from dead.

Kimball reported no baptisms from this church-planting venture. Ending his preaching in Sunderland void of immediate results probably did not surprise him. It was the first time that a Seventh-day Adventist preacher had attempted to branch out from Jamaica across the mountains directly into southwestern Vermont. Kimball characterized Sunderland as spiritually lax, an oblique reference to the possibility that Ethan Allen's century-old deist movement in this region surrounding Bennington may have long since become less aggressive, but it was far from dead.

Realizing that the Jamaica church was his first responsibility, Kimball changed his strategy, devoting more time to motivate members to become conscious of their own spiritual needs, to grow in faith, and to find ways to witness personally throughout southern Vermont. He apparently fulfilled his objective well. William Covert, an ordained minister coming from Michigan, found an active congregation when he began a six-day revival on January 18, 1893.

"This church has been organized over thirty years," Covert reflected, "yet there are those right in their midst who have recently embraced the message, and still others are interested." He baptized three and reclaimed wandering members, one returning with "confession and weeping." Interest in the church was spreading to the village of Jamaica, five miles distant, where Kimball and a church member planned to hold meetings.[14]

Similar to the experience of other Seventh-day Adventist churches in the United States before 1897, Jamaica's experiment with an elementary school was short-lived, but Kimball found other activities to promote. One was temperance, a national reform issue that was also of significant interest to Seventh-day Adventists. Kimball took the matter further than simply a pledge of abstinence from alcohol and tobacco. In his view, the notion of temperance applied to lifestyle in general and included diet. During the winter of 1892/1893, he organized a series of seminars to promote healthful eating habits, arguing that the "needs and desires of the flesh" directly influenced spirituality.

Forming a committee of church members to discuss specific phases of this question, Kimball led the church through reading assignments, discussion sessions, cooking classes, and even presentations about healthful dress. Promoting healthful living had become an Adventist passion, and Kimball, perhaps with great pleasure, excoriated practices such as excessive use of fats and sugar and baking with white flour instead of wheat flour. No one could accuse him of selling the Scripture short as he connected his points to the Bible. In fact, he predicated his entire project on the biblical injunction to be temperate in all things.

Kimball had never heard of wellness, a popular twentieth-century term that described how one was to maintain a healthful lifestyle. But he understood the principle and did not hesitate to portray it as a spiritual obligation. Enthusiastically reporting his meetings, he said that some who had given no thought to such matters had become "strongly biased for the right," some of whom might even carry the "light to the darkest points of earth."[15]

Kimball's pastoral activities took effect. When Covert, now the newly-elected president of the Vermont Conference, returned to Jamaica in October 1893, to conduct a quarterly meeting, he witnessed the addition of seventeen members, the largest one-time increase in the history of the congregation. With this boost, membership topped out at ninety-nine,[16] which, without a doubt, made the Jamaica church the largest Seventh-day Adventist congregation in the Vermont Conference.

The Impact of the Jamaica Church on Southern Vermont

It was evident to the conference president that Kimball's work in Jamaica was rippling over much of southern Vermont. Before reaching Jamaica, Covert visited a family of eight in Windham that had begun to observe the Saturday Sabbath. Kimball had made the original contact with them and asked Covert to talk with them.

Traveling to Wilmington in the southern reaches of the county, Covert also called on another family of six who had "embraced the truth" largely because of the work of colporteurs from the Jamaica church. Windham and Wilmington, separated by about thirty miles with Jamaica sandwiched between them, were "outposts of the Jamaica church," Covert affirmed.[17]

Covert himself followed with evangelistic meetings in Windham. He finished in November and organized a church of twenty-two. To reach this total, eleven transferred from the Jamaica church because Windham was closer to their home.[18] Years earlier, Saturday Sabbath keepers in Andover had been members of the Jamaica congregation, but they preferred to meet by themselves. In 1881, they became members of the newly organized Andover-Weston church. After the group in Windham became an official church, the Jamaica members could make a case that they had helped to spawn two new churches.

The conversion of the family in Wilmington illustrated the extent to which leaders of individual congregations depended on colporteurs to spread Adventism. At the time, literature sales probably received more promotion than any other activity in the churches. Colporteurs did not receive a salary from church funds but lived on sales commissions. In the eyes of church leaders, they were church "workers," salaried or not, because of the nature of their tasks.

In 1890, Bicknell handed off his responsibility as state agent to F. S. Porter. The new leader responded by offering training sessions, one of them in Jamaica in November of that year. Announcing that he would devote two days to this task, he added that he would stay as long "as the interest and the work demand."[19] Because many from the Jamaica church had already joined this work, Porter's meetings did not introduce anything new. Two-and-a-half years later, a conference announcement of a Bible institute in Jamaica for church workers in southern Vermont suggested the impact that colporteurs were having. The two-week schedule included two Bible studies each day and instruction in sales skills.[20] Seventeen attended another institute in Jamaica the next year, ten of whom contracted to work in Bennington and Windham counties.[21]

No one could doubt the importance of colporteur activity to church outreach in southern Vermont after Covert disclosed that in June 1894, conference leaders would hold a camp meeting in South Londonderry for members in the region. However, he made it clear that the annual business session would take place later at the traditional camp meeting in the north.²² About 150 attended the event in the south, and on the weekends, crowds came from the local community.²³ In 1895, the conference repeated the gathering in the same location.²⁴ The president's report of the meetings omitted any reference to Jamaica, but this large church was still the centerpiece of Seventh-day Adventism in southern Vermont, although it was no longer the sole locus of church activity.

A. S. Hutchins, who had served the Jamaica Adventists with commitment and paternal care since the days when they were still called Millerites and Sabbatarians, had done as much as anyone to set the stage for membership growth in southern Vermont. Pragmatically, he had also advised that Seventh-day Adventists must have a regional rather than a local presence in the south before assigning a resident pastor to southern Vermont. It was on his influence and work that others had capitalized.

Hutchins lived to see Adventism in southern Vermont end its existence as a dangling appendage to conference activity and become a partner with the northern part of the state. But on June 20, 1894, only three days before the first camp meeting in South Londonderry began, he passed away in Essex Junction.²⁵ An era had ended.

Notes

1. "Vermont," *RH*, October 6, 1885.
2. "Kimball" (Obituary), *RH*, July 4, 1929.
3. "Vermont," *RH*, February 10, 1885.
4. "Vermont," *RH*, March 24, 1885.
5. "Vermont Conference Report," *RH*, October 7, 1884; "Vermont Conference Proceedings," *RH*, October 6, 1885.
6. "Death of Elder A. S. Hutchins," *RH*, July 17, 1894.
7. "Vermont," *RH*, March 2, 1886; "How to Use Clubs of 'Signs' in Vermont," ibid.
8. "Vermont Tract Society Proceedings," *RH*, September 14, 1886.
9. See pastoral reports in *RH*, October 6, 1885; March 2, 1886; March 29, 1887; March 6, 1888.
10. "Vermont," *RH*, March 29, 1887.
11. "The Canvassing Work in Vermont," *RH*, November 19, 1889.
12. "Addresses," *RH*, March 29, 1892.
13. "Vermont," *RH*, July 5, 1892.
14. "Vermont," *RH*, February 7, 1893.
15. "Temperance Meetings at Jamaica, Vt.," *RH*, June 13, 1893.
16. "Vermont," *RH*, October 24, 1893.

17. Ibid.
18. "Vermont," *RH*, November 28, 1893.
19. "Appointments," *RH*, November 15, 1890.
20. "Vermont," *RH*, May 30, 1893.
21. "Vermont," *RH*, May 8. 1894.
22. "Southern Vermont Camp-Meeting," *RH*, May 29, 1894.
23. "Southern Vermont Camp-Meeting," *RH*, June 17, 1894.
24. "Vermont Local Camp-Meeting," *RH*, July 23, 1895.
25. An untitled news note, *RH*, June 26, 1894; *RH*, July 17, 1894.

Early Sabbatarian Adventist Families in Jamaica

So who were the people who constituted the Seventh-day Adventist Church in Jamaica, Vermont? The early members have long since passed on to their final rest, and no membership lists or church records remain to tell us who they were and what they did. Only a few names appear in news stories and obituaries, but even the most informative of these are sketchy.

The Meaning and Practice of Membership

In addition to the absence of data, a definition of Sabbatarian membership is problematic before 1860, the year when the name *Seventh-day Adventist* became official. Before that date, anyone who appeared in the Sabbatarian press as "brother" or "sister" from Jamaica was not by definition a baptized believer of Sabbatarianism, because Sabbatarian leaders addressed all Christians in this manner.

The nature of membership also posed complex problems. By 1850, belief in the second advent and observance of the Saturday Sabbath had become the central doctrines in a body of teachings that formed the basis for Sabbatarian identity. Ministers baptized converts who adopted these beliefs, but these sheep were members of their immediate flock only. *Denominational* membership was not possible, because a legally recognized church did not exist. Rather than a symbol of denominational membership, baptism was a mark of personal identification for those who observed Saturday and believed in the second advent.

A recognized denomination did not exist, because leaders of the Sabbatarian movement did not want to organize one.

A recognized denomination did not exist because leaders of the Sabbatarian movement did not want to organize one. Their sentiments derived from a combination of influences. An ingrained suspicion of organized religion pervaded their thinking. After the Great Disappointment in 1844, they had become prominent in the movement by rising to the top, having established themselves not by authority vested in them by an incorporated church but on the strength of their personalities, persuasive power, and their conviction that they were divinely led. In general, Sabbatarian believers accepted these conditions of leadership. Forming congregations was as far as these leading personalities wanted to carry organization. To a degree, each Sabbatarian congregation was a law unto itself.

Such nebulous views of organization were in keeping with anti-formalism, a pietist residue of Millerism, which was a trans-denominational movement, not an organized church. Miller himself encouraged his followers to maintain their conviction about a literal, premillennial return of Jesus to this earth but to remain members in their own churches. However, the excommunication of Millerites before 1844 showed that premillennialism could not coexist with postmillennialism, the prevailing theology of the times. The strength of convictions on both sides of the excommunication struggle led premillennialists to regard organized churches as Babylon and laid a footing for antagonism toward forming a legally incorporated church.

But organization could not remain irrelevant indefinitely. By 1850, Sabbatarians adopted a set of beliefs that defined their distinctiveness more sharply than ever. However loosely organized the Sabbatarians wished to remain, ministerial reports in the *Review* indicated that through the 1850s, Sabbatarians not only baptized believers but also ordained their ministers and disfellowshipped backsliders. Congregations operated with duly chosen leaders. These activities presupposed organizational authority, but such authority functioned because the rank and file voluntarily accepted leadership that was not institutionalized.

The number of Sabbatarians steadily increased during the 1850s. By the end of the decade, they realized that they had outgrown their movement and had become a *de facto* denomination that at the same time shunned organizational trappings. But without organization, there could be no universal statement of beliefs for Sabbatarians, and thus leaders had no official means to measure membership.

For those who had been part of the earlier Millerite movement, accepting the need for organization represented a 180-degree turnaround. On the occasion of their excommunication as Millerites, organization did not matter to them because they expected shortly to dwell in paradise, but by establishing belief in the second advent as a test of faith, they laid the cornerstone for a future separate communion.[1]

The concept of membership started to change after 1860, when Sabbatarians began the process of organization that they completed in 1863. Baptism now carried a denominational meaning, and membership became subject to a disciplined definition that a central organization controlled. However, membership itself was still determined at the congregational level; consequently, organization did not equate to uniformity among congregations or individual believers, but organizing a denomination made it possible to unify members and membership in ways that had been lacking before organization occurred.

For Sabbatarians, adopting a legal name with authority to own property, incorporate institutions, and establish doctrinal orthodoxy did not unleash a stampede among believers to accept a newer concept of membership. We may safely guess that many Sabbatarian Adventists clung to their earlier notions of membership after 1860. One of the tasks of Seventh-day Adventist ministers in the years immediately after 1860 was to convince Sabbatarians that membership should complement belief because they represented two sides of the same coin.

During a visit to Braintree, Vermont, in 1868, A. C. Bourdeau appealed to "certain ones present who had kept the Sabbath, and had been friendly to the cause for several years, but they had not as yet united with any church." Bourdeau hoped that they would "fully identify themselves with the people of God."[2] Overtones of the meaning of denominational membership were close to the surface of Bourdeau's comments.

Stephen Pratt

Among the Sabbatarians in the Jamaica area who came out of the Millerite movement was Stephen Pratt. We do not know if he was ever a member of the Pikes Falls congregation, but he was a believer who journeyed from Millerism to Sabbatarianism and, finally, to Seventh-day Adventism. Born in 1818 at Sandgate, Vermont, about twenty miles west of Jamaica near the New York line, he appears to have been in or around Jamaica when he became a Millerite in 1844. How intimately he was involved in the frenetic activity of some Millerites is an unanswered question, but he never seemed apologetic that local authorities locked him up in the county jail in their attempt to break up the gatherings of those who preached the second advent.[3]

Realizing that Jamaica was a difficult place for believers to maintain their beliefs, and seeking a source of encouragement, in 1854, Pratt encouraged James White to arrange a visit by a Sabbatarian minister to the community. Practicing his faith in a discouraging environment was not the only hardship Pratt experienced. By 1858, his financial condition became dire. Owning only a cow, no more than four sheep, and a few farm fowl, and working only "on hire," his income was meager. Pratt was so hard put he could not afford a subscription to the *Review*, yet he had opened his home to his bed-ridden mother-in-law and two sisters-in-law, one with a terminal illness and the other also sick but trying to mother a two-year-old child. Sometimes the household went without food.

In a letter from Isaac Pike, news of Pratt's circumstances reached Battle Creek, Michigan, in 1858. James White responded with an editorial about the responsibility of Christians to the poor. He canceled the subscription bill he had sent to Pratt for the *Review* and ordered the publishing house to send a free subscription to the financially beleaguered brother. White also collected some cash to send to him and asked a Sabbatarian minister to investigate the situation and report back to the *Review* office.[4]

The outcome of that inquiry is lost, but Pratt's personal circumstances improved sufficiently to allow him to pay for denominational papers and books through the 1860s and into the 1870s.[5] It is doubtful that he ever developed skills for a specialized career. About 1880 he was living in nearby South Londonderry and still working as a common laborer.[6] The year 1904 found him in South Wardsboro. In the same year at age eighty-six, he became a member of the Seventh-day Adventist Church in Windham; whether he did so by baptism or by transferring from another church is not clear. He died in 1910, "one of the fast disappearing links connecting the 1844 movement with these times," S. A. Holden wrote.[7]

The Sage Family

Betsey Sage, the first Millerite in Jamaica whose name appeared in the Sabbatarian press, also traveled from Millerism to Sabbatarianism. She wrote that she and other Millerites in the area were "in darkness" before Frederick Wheeler explained the seventh-day Sabbath during his visit in 1852. The L. J. Sage who wrote Betsey's obituary was probably her daughter-in-law, Lois, who dated Betsey's Sabbatarianism a year earlier, from 1851.[8] The editor of the *Review* called Betsey "Sister Sage," but her name did not appear on the charter membership list of the Jamaica church that organized a decade after she made contact with the *Review*.

Betsey was in her ninety-ninth year before old age finally overcame her on January 18, 1878. Born in 1779 during the Revolutionary War, she was already in her mid-sixties in 1844 when she became a Millerite. At the time of her death, she suffered from dementia and did not recognize her own children. Her survivors represented a prolific posterity. Starting with seven children, they included forty grandchildren, seventy great-grandchildren, and five great-great-grandchildren.[9]

The *Review* carried Betsey's obituary, which described her as a faithful believer but did not state that she was a member of the Jamaica congregation. At best, we can only conjecture that before her mind failed, she consummated her Sabbatarianism by sealing her membership in the Seventh-day Adventist Church.

Betsey was one of a well-known family in Jamaica. To the south of the Seventh-day Adventist meetinghouse, the peak of Sage Hill rose more than 2,000 feet, its southern slopes descending into the hamlet of West Jamaica. Several Sage families lived in the shadow of this hill during the 1860s, but Betsey's son, Emery, and Emery's wife, Martha, lived a few miles away, north of the meetinghouse.[10]

The "sudden and terrible death of Bro. E. [Emery] Sage's only son" on August 2, 1868, "brought deep affliction upon this entire church," A. C. Bourdeau wrote during his visit to Pikes Falls in October and November, following the tragedy.[11] He and his wife had traveled from northern Vermont to Jamaica to conduct their pastoral rounds. More than two months after young Sage's death, they found church members still so shaken that most congregational activities were at near standstill. Bourdeau did not detail how the fourteen-year-old had died, but he observed that the circumstances of the death made the occasion especially difficult.

Emery and Martha Sage continued to know sadness. In 1875, seven years after their son's untimely death, five of their daughters were baptized together and joined the Jamaica church. Among them was Abbie, at the time twenty-four years old. A year later Abbie enrolled in the first Seventh-day Adventist post-secondary institution, Battle Creek College, in Battle Creek, Michigan. After two terms of study, she landed a teaching position in Michigan, but her new career did not last long. In the fall of 1878, Abbie returned to Jamaica, where she spent the final year of her life, a victim of tuberculosis. R. S. Owen said she "bore her affliction with Christian fortitude."[12]

Six years later in 1885, Rhoda, the youngest of Abbie's sisters who had shared the same baptismal day, also passed away. Like Abbie, Rhoda lost her battle against tuberculosis. Her short life had been far from pleasant. Two-and-a-half years before her death, her husband died. The stress proved too much to bear, and her mind became "deranged," her obituary said. Treatments revived her, but her weakened body could not resist the pneumonia that she contracted shortly before her death. When she succumbed, she left a two-year-old son, now orphaned.[13]

Too often, parents in the Adventist community buried their children. James and Rosina Wilder lost a son, sixteen-year-old Clarke, to typhoid fever in 1859. With their other sons, Jared and David, they became charter members of the Jamaica church in 1862. Only a year later the father died of heart disease, and three years after his death, nineteen-year-old David wrote the obituary for his twenty-one-year-old brother, Jared, who had also developed a fatal heart condition. After four more years elapsed, death struck again. David's child was found dead in bed.[14]

In 1863, D. W. and E. A. Johnson watched helplessly as their thirteen-year-old daughter, Carrie, died after a day-and-a-half of sickness. The grieving parents wrote that they were "not fully satisfied what the disease was" but prayed that God would "sanctify this most deep affliction" to their eternal good.[15] Over a three-year stretch from 1864 to 1867, C. N. and Emeline Pike, also charter members of the church, buried a son and a daughter, each less than two years old. At the time of their deaths, each baby was an only child.[16] Similarly, Emerson and Fidelia Edson saw their three-year-old son, Alfred, succumb to dysentery in 1877.[17] Much later, in 1893, Esther Aurelia, the eighteen-month-old daughter of Frank and Susie Bourn, fell to "brain fever," according to her obituary.[18]

It would be a time, they believed, when families, shattered by death, could expect restoration.

A common thread in these somber events was the reaction of bereaved parents and other relatives who expressed their strengthened hope in one of their central beliefs, the second advent. It would be a time, they believed, when families, shattered by death, could expect restoration. This tenet was crucial. It not only offered comfort but also played a fundamental role in shaping their spiritual identity.

Isaac Newton Pike and Health Reform

The passing of these children reveals that while Vermont was no longer the northern frontier that had once beckoned to adventurous settlers, it was apparent that since those early pioneer days, rural life had not yet become safe or easy. The frequency of sickness, and sometimes death, underscored the sobering truth that medical care, especially in the hinterlands, was still far short of safeguarding people against infections and life-threatening illness.

One Sabbatarian in Pikes Falls who committed himself to raising the level of public health was Isaac Newton Pike, who had lived in Jamaica since 1847. He operated a sawmill and a farm, was a surveyor, and practiced Thomsonian medicine. Some have added law to his skills as well. He was unquestionably the community patriarch.[19] He also acted the part of a local land tycoon.[20]

Pike's concern about his fellow believer, Stephen Pratt, was typical of many entries in his diary for the year 1869, which reveals him as a man busy with caring for the physical well-being of the community.[21] "Visited the sick," he scrawled for January 30, a phrase that appears frequently, suggesting that he took his responsibility as the resident medicine man seriously. He dispensed medicines, either by visiting homes or by selling them directly to neighbors who stopped by his house for advice. In January alone, three visitors each bought an ounce of paregoric.[22]

Pike's diary indicates that he kept on hand dosages of red precipitate, sulphur, senna, pink, extract of dandelion, pulmonary balsam, liquid cough medicine, cough drops, licorice, pain "annihilator," castor oil, black plaster, hemlock plaster, essence of peppermint, liniment, borax, catarrh root, and other unnamed pills.[23] His frequent application of such remedies as balsam, licorice, cough medicines, and catarrh root imply a high incidence of respiratory maladies, including tuberculosis, among his neighbors.

Not always did the sick whom Pike visited recover. During 1869, he noted that seven persons in the community died.[24] He had not treated all of them. "Leander Bourn had a boy born," he recorded on January 17. A week later he went to see Mary, the new mother, who was sick. Two days later, he stopped by the Bourns' house to see her again. That night she died, only nineteen years old. Her obituary said she was a "worthy member of the church."[25]

Pike did not explain her death, but the winter of 1869 was long and cold, and Mary died only nine days after bearing her son. The next day Pike took his compass to help look for a gravesite. We can guess that the place he marked was on the rise behind the yet unfinished meetinghouse, a spot in what would become a tiny cemetery for the church. Mary, whose real name was Marietta, was probably the first to be buried there. Ironically, according to the grave markers still standing in this cemetery, the last person interred in this small resting place was Henry K. Pike, one of Isaac's sons and husband to Sarah Bourn, Mary's older sister-in-law.[26]

As a practitioner of Thomsonian medicine, Pike was part of a nineteenth-century attempt to outflank conventional medicine with herbal extracts.

As a practitioner of Thomsonian medicine, Pike was part of a nineteenth-century attempt to outflank conventional medicine with herbal extracts. To become a Thomsonian doctor, one read an instructional manual about how to prepare medicines. By pledging to shroud these formulas with secrecy and paying $20, a buyer could peddle botanic remedies.[27] The Windham County business directory called Pike a "practicing physician of the Thompsonian [sic] school,"[28] which presupposed that he had gone through the necessary rituals to distribute medicines. Whatever Pike's credentials were, J. G. Eddy did not include him in the list of physicians who practiced medicine in Jamaica.[29]

But Pike did not restrict himself to Thomsonian sources for his medicines. On June 30, 1869, he traveled to Brattleboro, where he bought medicines at I. N. Thorn & Son, a pharmaceutical outlet dealing in botanical as well as conventional medications.[30] Pike did not hesitate to resort to other time-honored medicinal traditions, such as a quantity of metheglin that he provided to another neighbor.[31] When mixed with honey and allowed to ferment, the blend became an intoxicant, but before it acquired a tang, many drank the brew for medicinal purposes. Although not a medicine, a product that Pike also promoted was Graham flour, a baking item that reformer Sylvester Graham had popularized in the earlier part of the century.[32]

Pike depended on a variety of sources of information about health, primarily the Seventh-day Adventist health reform movement. In September 1866, the denomination founded the Western Health Reform Institute in Battle Creek, Michigan. A month before the Institute opened its doors, the denomination began to publish *The Health Reformer*, a monthly journal devoted to lifestyle changes that would contribute to healthful living. Pike subscribed to this periodical as well as to *Laws of Life*, a similar paper originating at Dr. James C. Jackson's "Our Home on the Hillside," a health resort in Dansville, New York. One of Jackson's specialties was water-cure treatments. Many Seventh-day Adventists were acquainted with "Our Home." Some, including James and Ellen White, had participated in its program.[33]

The ideas that Pike derived from the *Health Reformer* and *Laws of Life* helped him when dealing with both the technical and philosophical issues of health. The *Health Reformer* that Pike received on January 13, presumably the January copy, contained a technical article about sugar, followed by a discussion of the dangers of its use. Two articles condemning tobacco and alcohol, coupled with a discussion about temperance in diet, broadened the narrower view of temperance as a movement against alcohol consumption only. A short opinion piece about using simple remedies instead of drugs fit neatly into Pike's Thomsonian philosophy. A notable feature of the periodical was a column by Russell T. Trall, M. D., who helped to introduce water-cures to America and later established the New York Hygeia-Therapeutic College, which trained physicians with skills in hydrotherapy.[34]

Health reform enjoyed a warm reception among at least some in the Pikes Falls church. In the columns of the denomination's general paper, C. M. Nichols Jr., a church member and one of Jamaica's several mill owners, expressed his gratitude for the "laws of our being. The health reform has been a great blessing to me," he said. "For about three years we have been trying to live out its principles."[35] Isaac Pike's oldest child, Olive Knight, who appears repeatedly in her father's diary, also wrote that she was thankful for what she had "learned of the health reform, and especially for the dress reform."[36] Olive was also a user of Graham flour.[37]

Nichols's and Knight's vision of health reform as an integral part of Seventh-day Adventist lifestyle was a point that Isaac Sanborn brought with him when he arrived in Jamaica in 1878 to begin a six-month evangelistic campaign. For more than a dozen years before coming to Jamaica, he had personally tested health reform practice and promoted it with unapologetic ardor, even if it required dramatic change in his own habits. The critical issue was the results. Sanborn announced in 1867 that he had become a vegetarian, reduced food intake to two meals a day, ate bread baked from Graham flour, stopped drinking fluids with his meals, and quit using butter. He claimed not to have suffered a cold in two years and to have cured his rheumatism so he could walk without pain.[38] At the time he was about forty-five years old.

Although Sanborn did not report any attempt to lecture the Jamaica church about health reform, doubtless he kept neither his habits nor his convictions a secret. Whatever enthusiasm his personal experience may have generated in the Jamaica congregation, over the years interest in the rigors of health reform waned among some members. Sensing that the willingness of their spirit was no match against the weakness of their flesh, I. E. Kimball organized a series of health seminars for the Jamaica church in the winter of 1892/1893. His sessions discussed all of the topics that the Adventist health reformers had been advocating for more than twenty-five years.[39]

Despite Isaac Pike's interest in health reform, he did not seem ready to accept every piece of advice the *Health Reformer* and other sources recommended. Coffee and pork appear to have been part of his menu, both items that Seventh-day Adventist health protagonists in Battle Creek frowned upon.[40] Pike died in 1884 and so did not live to hear Kimball's seminars. We can surmise, however, that if Jamaica's Thomsonian practitioner had not altered some of his private habits that his diary implied, he would have been at odds with some of Kimball's positions.

Isaac Pike's Wide-Ranging Influence

Pike had an inquisitive mind and a penchant for books and periodicals. His reading habits reflected a desire to stay abreast of trends in health, the church, the Christian community in general, and the local scene as well. In addition to the two magazines about health, he subscribed to the *Advent Review and Sabbath Herald*. Also coming to his home were *The Christian* and *The Household*, two non-Adventist magazines, which suggests that he was willing to look beyond Seventh-day Adventist horizons for information and ideas.[41]

Pike repeatedly spent money on books and went out of his way to search for reading material. During 1869, he ordered numerous volumes from the Seventh-day Adventist publishing house in Michigan. On February 24, seven arrived at the same time. Once he purchased a book directly from D. M. Canright, a prominent Seventh-day Adventist minister who had been one of the principal speakers at the Vermont Conference camp meeting in 1868. Twice during the year, Pike paid a few cents for a *Testimony*, a small collection of special messages and counsel to church members published in booklet form in Battle Creek, Michigan. While on a business trip to Brattleboro, he purchased a book from Cheney & Clapp, booksellers.

Other purchases included some books from a family that was moving from Pikes Falls to the West. From a Mary E. Cox he also purchased sixteen physiology charts and several other volumes, among them books dealing with health, including obstetrics. He made an especially useful acquisition in February when the "Law book for the present year" arrived. He bought books from his daughter Olive and his son Henry, both living in Pikes Falls. Pike also acquired reading material from Cassius White, a member of the church. Some of his periodicals he bound into books.[42]

Like her father, Olive Knight was a reader. She passed literature on to him, and she read the *Review* regularly, which compensated for being "deprived of the privilege of meeting with the people of God on the Sabbath," she penned in a letter to church leaders in Battle Creek. Shortly before her letter appeared in the *Review*, her mother spent a Saturday with her, and on a later Saturday, Isaac said his wife babysat the Knight children so Olive could "go to meeting."[43]

How Pike found time to read these books and papers is an enigma, although he scratched in his diary that on many Saturdays he "staid [*sic*] home & read."[44] He did not often explain this alternative to the Sabbath services. On occasion he felt "unwell," but whatever his ailment, it was not serious enough to prevent him from reading. He also spent some Saturdays making his rounds among the sick,[45] a task that he sometimes could not wedge in between his responsibilities as a farmer and sawmill owner.

When the members of the Jamaica church began to erect their own meetinghouse in 1868, the membership exceeded thirty. No one kept an attendance record of their church services, but until their new sanctuary was ready for occupation, they met in homes. O. A. Richmond and Emery Sage, both living in the vicinity of the yet uncompleted church, welcomed the members to their homes on several Saturdays. Except for one Saturday, the members met at Isaac Pike's house from April 24 to May 29.

Once at another home, Pike read the sermon at what probably was an evening gathering.[46] Occasionally, he attended a midweek prayer meeting.[47]

Pike did not describe the format of worship services without a minister, but the members probably followed a simple service as they fended for themselves without pastoral leadership. Pike's diary implies that A. S. Hutchins's visit in July 1869, was the only one that year by an ordained minister.[48] While in Jamaica, Hutchins conducted a memorial service for Marietta Bourn, who had died six months earlier.[49]

Construction on the Jamaica meetinghouse began after Abraham Bourn donated the land. Bourn's wife, Catherine, was a daughter of Betsey Sage as well as a charter member of the Jamaica church. The congregation expected that members would donate labor and funds.

A. C. Bourdeau, who had encouraged the members to build, noted in June 1868, that they had "made a start in getting out some timber for their meetinghouse," but the project had stalled. Bourdeau did not disclose where the lumber originated, but with two owners of sawmills in the congregation—Isaac Pike and Charles Nichols—the question of lumber for construction should not have been problematic.[50]

Whether Pike helped with the lumber is a lost detail, but he recorded that he supported the meetinghouse in other ways. After Bourdeau and his wife promoted the construction project during a pastoral visit in November 1868, Pike took them to the train station in Manchester, a circuitous, twenty-mile carriage trip across the mountains that required them to set out at 4:00 a.m.[51]

Credit: Russell Pike

Silas Pike (1841-1923), seventh child and fifth son of Isaac and Jane Pike. Silas spent most of his life in or near Pikes Falls. Two of his grandsons, Carroll and Victor, were ordained ministers and pastored in Pikes Falls during the 1930s and 1940s.

Twice in March, Pike went to the meetinghouse for unspecified reasons. In April he worked parts of two days on the church, and on a Sunday he helped unload brick. He paid for the paint and the songbooks and helped to install the stove. Construction was far enough along for the members to conduct their first Sabbath services in the meetinghouse on August 14. Pike spent nearly ten hours at the church during the next two days, working first "for Cassius White" on Sunday and the next morning on the pews.[52] From August 14 forward, Pike does not mention gatherings in homes, which implies that the weekly worship service continued in the new meetinghouse.

Pike expressed no political views in his diary, but he was a civic-minded person. Before moving to Jamaica, he lived in Stratton, a stronghold of the Whig Party and site of the Whig convention in 1840. Six days after renowned United States Senator Daniel Webster addressed this gathering, Pike's wife, Jane, bore her fourth son, whom the parents named Daniel Webster Pike. At the time, Isaac was one of Stratton's three selectmen.[53] Before this event, he served as justice of the peace in Stratton and constable in Somerset.[54]

Pike's diary shows that he regularly attended the school meeting of his local district in Jamaica. He also drew plans for a new post office in Jamaica and helped to prepare the documents that the federal government required to establish a post office. In February 1869, he wrote to an unidentified jailor, and two-and-a-half-months later in April he "was called" to Newfane, about fifteen miles south of Jamaica, where he "went in the Jail to see the prisoners."[55] Pike did not reveal if the trip was a result of his letter, nor did he explain his trip, but we may conjecture that the reason for his visit was to offer medical advice or to offer simple treatments to inmates.

There is no way to measure the intangible benefits the Jamaica church enjoyed from Pike's influence, but there is little doubt that his connections were an advantage to the congregation. He also taught his family the duty of civic responsibility. Calvin N. Pike, sometimes called C. N. Pike, the third son of Isaac and Jane, served as one of the selectmen of Stratton from 1881 through 1888, except for one year, 1887. He also served as town treasurer for two years, 1890 and 1891.[56]

From the outset the Jamaica church was a family affair.

From the outset the Jamaica church was a family affair. The nine charter members in 1862 were Catherine Bourn; Henry K. Pike and his wife, Sarah; Calvin N. Pike and his wife, Emeline; and James and Rosina Wilder and their two sons, Jared and David. Besides being the daughter of Betsey Sage, Catherine Bourn was the mother of Sarah Pike, Henry's wife. Emeline Pike was the daughter of James and Rosina Wilder and a sister to Jared and David. Henry and Calvin Pike were brothers. Catherine Bourn and Rosina Wilder were sisters. Also, the families of O. A. Richmond and Charlie Nichols, both of whom hosted church services in their homes during 1869, were related. Emery Sage was a brother to Catherine Bourn and Rosina Wilder.[57] These families lived in proximity to the meetinghouse in either the Jamaica or Stratton sections of Pikes Falls. Isaac Pike frequently visited their homes.

Pike's name does not appear among the charter members of the Jamaica church, but he left his mark on both the community and the Seventh-day Adventist Church. Since his death in 1884, he has rested in the tiny cemetery behind the Pikes Falls meetinghouse. His three surviving sons in 1869, Henry, Calvin, and Silas, all of whom appear in his diary, were active church members who passed their faith on to their children. At the Vermont Conference session in 1882, Henry served on the auditing committee.[58] In 1887, Calvin received a colporteur's license.[59] From Silas' descendants came two ordained ministers, Carroll and Victor.[60]

In addition to these few families, the names of later members also appear in connection with the church. Some of them were from older families in Jamaica; others moved into the community. We know little about them, but a few left enough tracks to follow their trail. The records they left are no less fascinating than those of the original families.

Notes

1. David Rowe writes the following: "By 1843 it was apparent that Millerism was developing its own personality, quite distinct from its quality as a revivalist movement" (*Thunder and Trumpets*, p. 49). Rowe's statement appears to contradict his earlier observation that I have cited in the chapter "Millerite Background" of this study, which declares that the Millerite movement was devoid of personality. See Rowe's discussion of the origin of denominationalism among Millerites in *Thunder and Trumpets,* pp. 115–118.
2. "Report from Bro. A. C. Bourdeau," *RH*, April 7, 1868.

3. "Aged Pilgrims," *Gleaner*, March 30, 1904; "Obituary Notices," *Gleaner*, August 24, 1910. D. K. Young, *Echoes in the Forest* (Stratton: Town of Stratton, 2000), pp. 396–398 discusses the Pratt family as one-time residents of Stratton but does not mention the Stephen Pratt appearing in this narrative.
4. "The Poor," *RH*, April 15, 1858; news announcement, *RH*, May 13, 1858.
5. The editor of the *Review* published the names of those who subscribed to the paper as well as purchased books or sent money to the denominational headquarters. Pratt's name appears regularly as a subscriber. See *RH*, 1860s, 1870s, passim.
6. Hamilton Child, ed., *Gazetteer and Business Directory of Windham County, Vt. 1724–1884* (Syracuse, NY: Journal Office, 1884), p. 428. Although Pratt was living in South Londonderry, Child included him in the list of residents of Jamaica. Hereafter this source cited as *Gazetteer*.
7. "Obituary Notices," *Gleaner*, August 24, 1910.
8. "Obituary Notices," *RH*, February 28, 1878. See Betsey Sage's letter, *RH*, January 20, 1853.
9. "Obituary Notices," *RH*, February 28, 1878.
10. Maps of Jamaica township from Beer's *Atlas* supplied to Floyd Greenleaf by Sophia Sanderson, assistant town clerk of Jamaica, August 31, 2007. For genealogical information about the Sage family, see Young, *Echoes,* pp. 430, 431.
11. "The Cause in Jamaica, Vt.," *RH*, November 17, 1868. See also Jamaica Town Records.
12. "Obituary Notices," *RH*, November 20, 1879; "Report of Meetings in Vermont," *RH*, July 15, 1875.
13. Ibid.; "Obituary Notices," *RH*, June 23, 1885.
14. "Obituary Notices," *RH*, January 5, 1860; "Obituary Notices," *RH*, December 29, 1863; "Obituary Notices," *RH*, October 30, 1866. See Pike Diary, November 26.
15. "Obituary Notices," *RH*, March 3, 1863.
16. "Obituary Notices," *RH*, September 27, 1864; "Obituary Notices," *RH*, March 10, 1868.
17. "Obituary Notices," *RH*, October 4, 1877.
18. "Obituary Notices," *RH*, November 28, 1893. *Brain fever* was a nineteenth-century term for any one of several inflammations, including meningitis.
19. I have depended on Young, *Echoes*, pp. 370–383, for biographical data about the Pike family. Also see *Gazetteer*, pp. 235, 236. Pike recorded

in his diary that he surveyed land. See his entries for April 5, 9, and May 16. In 1856 the Vermont General Assembly passed a miscellaneous bill authorizing a payment to Pike for $6.25 for surveying a part of the boundary between Bennington and Windham counties. *The Acts and Resolves Passed by the General Assembly of the State of Vermont at the October Session, 1856* (Montpelier: E. P. Walton Jr.: 1856), p. 209.
20. After perusing land records of Jamaica, Charles Marchant believes that Isaac Pike owned vast acreage in the area, which agrees with the statement in *Gazetteer*, p. 235. Charles Marchant, telephone interview by Floyd Greenleaf, December 6, 2007. Young states that Isaac practiced law as evidenced by the land records of Jamaica (*Echoes*, p. 375). Warren E. Booker says that Isaac was also a surveyor (*Historical Notes*, p. 137).
21. Pike Diary.
22. Pike Diary, January 10, 26, and 27.
23. For entries about medicines, see Pike Diary, February 8, 9; March 6, 14, 15, 20, 21, 24, 31; April 3, 11; June 20; July 6; September 28; December 7.
24. Pike Diary, January 26; February 27; April 16; July 18; October 4; November 26; December 9.
25. Pike Diary, January 17, 24, 26. "Obituary Notices," *RH*, August 24, 1869.
26. Pike Diary, January 27, 28. See Charles Marchant's note about the cemetery behind the meetinghouse that he added to the end of Isaac Pike's diary. The cold winter of 1868/1869 extended well into April. As late as April 15, 1869, Pike measured five feet, four inches of snow on the "East side of the hill." Pike Diary, April 15. On each of the preceding nine days, Pike noted that the morning temperatures were below freezing, some mornings as low as 20°F.
27. Ronald L. Numbers, *Prophetess of Health: A Study of Ellen G. White* (New York: Harper and Row, 1976), pp. 6, 62.
28. *Gazetteer*, pp. 335, 336. Although the *Gazetteer* called Pike a practicing physician, he does not appear on the list of physicians for Windham County (*Gazetteer*, pp. 604, 605).
29. J. G. Eddy, "Jamaica," *VHG*, vol. 5, p. 431.
30. Pike Diary, June 30.
31. Pike Diary, July 5.
32. Entries on January 14, February 17, and May 20 all record sales of Graham flour.

33. Pike Diary entries for January 13, February 6, February 24. See Numbers, *Prophetess,* pp. 102–128.
34. *The Health Reformer* (January 1869). Trall warned about sugar on pp. 133, 134. The discussion about simple home remedies for maladies appears on pp. 138, 139. For Trall's experience with water-cure, see Numbers, *Prophetess*, pp. 64–67, 107–109.
35. "Extracts from Letters," *RH*, November 20, 1866.
36. Olive S. Knight to Uriah Smith, n.d. Published in *RH*, July 6, 1868.
37. Pike Diary, January 14.
38. Isaac Sanborn, "My Experience," *The Health Reformer* (January 1867), p. 84.
39. "Temperance Meetings at Jamaica, Vt.," *RH*, June 13, 1893.
40. Pike Diary, May 6, August 16.
41. Pike Diary, January 13, 14; February 24; March 26; July 12, 30; August 23; September 5.
42. Pike Diary, January 20; February 3, 9, 24, 26; March 2, 17; April 7, 8; June 30; August 23; September 23; October 1; December 14; January 2, 1870. Pike ended his diary on January 4, 1870.
43. O. S. Knight to *Review, RH*, March 9, 1869; Pike Diary, February 13; March 13.
44. Pike Diary, March 13; April 17; July 10, 17; August 7, 21.
45. Pike Diary, January 16, 30; February 6; March 6, 27.
46. Pike Diary, March 20; April 10, 24; May 8, 15, 22, 29; June 12; July 3, 24, 31.
47. Pike Diary, September 21 and November 16.
48. Pike Diary, July 24.
49. "Obituary Notices," *RH*, August 24, 1869.
50. "Report from Bro. A. C. Bourdeau," *RH*, August 18, 1868; Young, *Echoes*, pp. 56, 57. Besides Pike, O. A. Richmond operated a sawmill that Charles Nichols, Jr. later purchased. See *Gazetteer*, pp. 224, 428. Nichols's wife, Sarah, appears to have been a sister to O. A. Richmond. See Young, *Echoes*, p. 347.
51. "Report from A. C. Bourdeau," *RH*, December 1, 1868.
52. Pike Diary, March 17, 23; April 1, 2, 4; May 14; June 23; August 14, 22, 23; December 31. Cassius White was a new member who had moved to Pikes Falls the previous year.
53. D. K. Young, *The History of Stratton* (Stratton: Town of Stratton, 2001), pp. 138, 157–163; Young, *Echoes*, p. 375.

54. *Journal of the General Assembly of the State of Vermont for the Session Begun in 1835* (Middlebury, VT: Knapp and Jewett, 1835), p. 46; *VHG*, vol. 5, p. 531.
55. Pike Diary, February 5; March 30; April 18, 19; June 8; November 15, 16; December 15, 27.
56. Young, *History*, pp. 139, 142.
57. To trace the relationships among these families, I have depended on the Jamaica Town Records and passages devoted to these specific families in Young, *Echoes*.
58. "Vermont Conference," *RH*, September 26, 1882.
59. "Vermont Conference Proceedings," *RH*, October 11, 1887.
60. Obituary for Roy Ellsworth Pike, "At Rest," *Gleaner*, May 13, 1975. Roy Pike was the grandson of Silas Pike.

Later Adventist Families

Among the newcomers who moved to the area specifically to join the Jamaica church were William and Melissa White from Fairfield in northern Vermont. They settled in the Stratton section of Pikes Falls in 1868.[1] The Whites had become Seventh-day Adventists in 1864 and attended the Enosburgh church,[2] less than ten miles from their home. Because of the church's location in the hamlet of Bordoville, it was also known as the Bordoville church, the home congregation of the families of A. C. and D. T. Bourdeau, brothers and prominent Seventh-day Adventist ministers.

The White Family

As fellow congregants of the Bourdeaus, the Whites had no doubt heard accounts of the church in Jamaica. It does not appear merely coincidental that as A. C. Bourdeau became increasingly engaged in church affairs in Jamaica where the congregation was faltering on its commitment to follow through on its construction program, that the Whites threw themselves into the mix of events in southern Vermont. William and Melissa White had helped to build the church in Bordoville. Although William was in his mid-fifties in 1868, and Melissa about ten years younger, the experience of working on the meetinghouse energized them for more involvement in church affairs.

The Whites made an exploratory trip to Jamaica in October 1868, accompanying A. C. Bourdeau and his wife, who were paying a pastoral visit to southern Vermont. Because of heavy emigration, property in that part of Windham County was selling at bargain prices. The Whites bought a farm that once belonged to a Kidder family in the Stratton portion of Pike's Falls near the Jamaica church.[3] Almost immediately after the purchase, the Whites returned north to prepare for their move, but not before "liberally" donating funds to complete the meetinghouse, Bourdeau wrote. According to the lone document that survives the early period of the Jamaica church, William White gave $40 to pay for the stove and pipes.[4]

The Whites' decision to move south was more than a choice by William and Melissa. Their oldest son, Cassius, also was party to their commitment to Jamaica. In the summer of 1868, he was in Pikes Falls also and helped Bourdeau frame up and enclose the new meetinghouse.[5] Before the project ended, not only Cassius but eventually also his younger brothers, Flavius and Leslie, pitched in by actually working on construction and purchasing some of the furnishings.[6] After working with Bourdeau during the summer, Cassius continued donating time and effort to the meetinghouse, purchasing songbooks and items for use in the Sabbath school.[7]

Credit: Jamaica Historical Foundation

The three children of Cassius (1844-1901) and Louisa E. White, all born in Jamaica, Vermont. Left to right, Julius, Edith, and Hubert. The sons took over the management of the White Mop Wringer Company in 1901. Julius (1878-1955) served the Seventh-day Adventist church at administrative levels in the United States and China.

The facts we know about Cassius portray him as an energetic and innovative young man. He arrived in Jamaica in his mid-twenties, still single. From a local family he found a wife, Louisa Twitchell, whom he married on Christmas Day, 1872.[8] Five years later in 1877, he built a water-powered mill in Jamaica to manufacture shingles and butter tubs. Later he converted his business into a mop wringer manufacturing company. In 1891, he applied for a patent for a wringer that he had invented, but the US Patent Office received applications for seven wringers that year and delayed action on White's request. Not to be outdone by his competition, he filed his application again in 1894 and received a patent.[9]

The mop wringer enterprise succeeded well. Named the White Mop Wringer Company, it became one of the many small industries that fed the local Jamaica economy. Hubert and Julius, sons of Cassius and Louisa, took charge of the enterprise in 1901. Four years later, they transferred the business to Fultonville, New York, on the Erie Canal.[10] With them went other members of the Jamaica church, among them their cousin, Ina May Botsford, and her family. This move benefitted the company, but it drained relatively well-off members from the congregation. The loss of the factory was also part of the economic decline in Jamaica during the late nineteenth and early twentieth centuries that Mark Worthen describes.[11]

It is open to question whether the White family was unanimous about their move from Fairfield to Pikes Falls in 1868. Lester W., another son of William and Melissa, did not become a member of the church until 1877, nine years after the family moved. However, once he made his decision, he gave no one any reason to doubt his commitment. Julius, his nephew, praised his loyalty to the church in "influence, efforts, and means." For many years Lester White was a local elder of the church, the most elevated leadership position within the congregation.[12]

The White family contributed consistently to the local church and the Vermont Conference. At the annual session of the Vermont Conference in 1885, the delegates chose Flavius White, the youngest of William and Melissa's children, to serve on the committee to nominate conference officers and leaders of statewide church activities for the ensuing year.[13] It was the most influential committee of the conference business session. Two years later delegates named Flavius to be a member of the camp meeting committee.[14] In 1892, Cassius also served on the conference camp meeting committee.[15]

At the 1901 conference session, delegates elected J. G. White from Jamaica to serve as a field secretary in charge of a newly created conference department to promote Sabbath school activities throughout the state.[16] J. G. White was actually twenty-three-year-old Julius Gilbert White, Cassius and Louisa's son, born in Jamaica in 1878.[17] But Julius' new position did not make him a church employee. The impoverished conference treasury could not afford full-time ministers to oversee all conference projects and activities, which forced the nominating committee to turn to willing lay members to conduct the business of the church in Vermont.

Nevertheless, the 1901 conference session launched young White into a career of church service. As the session opened, he was appointed to the committee on nominations. Before the session ended, the delegates not only named him to oversee the Sabbath schools in Vermont but also chose him to be one of four delegates from Vermont to the business session of the newly organized union of conferences in northeastern United States.[18]

At the time, Julius, or J. G., as he was more commonly known by then, was intimately involved in the mop wringer business, but in 1902 he sandwiched in a Sabbath school convention in Rutland and, by special appointment, became a member of the conference executive committee.[19] His activity for the Vermont Conference impressed conference leaders. In 1902 they reinstated the church district system, which had long since fallen into disuse after A. C. Bourdeau initiated it in 1867. This action inspired J. G. White to jettison his responsibilities in the conference Sabbath school department to became a lay pastor of churches and companies of believers in Windsor and Windham counties.[20]

White's participation in church work took a detour in 1905 when he and his brother moved with the mop wringer business to New York.[21] Shortly, however, he volunteered for church projects again, finally selling the family business to become a full-time salaried employee of the denomination. Eventually, the White Mop Wringer Company became a subsidiary of the Electrolux corporation.[22] J. G. White died in 1955 after fulfilling many years of service to Seventh-day Adventist institutions, including a term of mission service in China.[23]

Before the White Mop Wringer Company transferred to New York, the White family had already begun to scatter from Jamaica. Leslie moved to Holyoke, Massachusetts.[24] Flavius also lived in Holyoke for a time but returned to southern Vermont, finally settling in West Dummerston.[25] Lester established a home in Winhall (after 1888 known as Bondville), in Bennington County but next door to Jamaica and Stratton, and later moved to Northfield, Vermont, before joining other members of his family, including his daughter, in Fultonville, New York.[26] William, the father, died in Holyoke, Massachusetts, in 1890.[27] Two years later Cassius's wife, Louisa, passed away while under hospital treatment in Worcester, Massachusetts,[28] and Melissa died in 1900 at the home of her son, Lester, in Northfield, Vermont.[29] Cassius passed away in December 1901.[30] Few families had contributed as much as the Whites to the Jamaica church.

The Twing Family

Another family that stood out in the Jamaica church was the Walter and Elizabeth Twing household, with their three sons. Walter and his brother, Luke, two of eleven children born to Samuel and Julia Twing, moved to southern Vermont shortly after 1910. The Twings had lived in the western regions of both Massachusetts and Connecticut.[31] Like many other small pieces of information, what motivated the Twings to move to Pikes Falls has disappeared from family lore. Early nineteenth-century censuses show some Twings living in Jamaica. Whether it was a family connection that Walter and Luke were renewing or the attraction of a well-known church that drew the two brothers to Jamaica, is not known. Whatever their reason, their arrival was a belated example of the migration flow up the Connecticut River Valley into Vermont that had begun during the late eighteenth century.

Before moving to Jamaica, Walter had worked several years as a baker at the Seventh-day Adventist New England Sanitarium in Melrose, Massachusetts, less than ten miles north of Boston.[32] Once in Vermont, he and his wife, Elizabeth, set up housekeeping in Stratton, but later moved to Jamaica near the Pikes Falls church. By 1912, he became the head elder of the congregation.[33]

Walter Twing's influence on the church was bold and long. As the leader of the church, he often became its spokesman and the person with whom conference leaders communicated. He met visiting conference officers at the train in Jamaica and sometimes entertained them in his home. More than once he wrote to a state official in Montpelier to solicit funds for church charities.[34]

Besides working their farm, Walter also trekked through southern Vermont peddling denominational literature.[35] After attending a rally in Burlington at the beginning of 1916, he set a goal of $800 in gross sales for the year.[36] His sales reports do not indicate that he was amassing wealth as a literature salesman, but no one could question his dedication.

Walter Twing's commitment to the church and his reverence for the Sabbath were bywords in Pikes Falls. Helen and Scott Nearing, neighbors, internationally known critics of the corporate world, and promoters of a simple, self-sufficient lifestyle, remembered Twing as someone who was "accommodating" and who "always went out of his way to be friendly." The Nearings frequently mixed concrete for construction projects on their homestead, but they knew it was out of the question even to ask to dig for sand in Twing's sand pit on Saturday.

> *A story that, according to the Nearings, was only a "tradition in the valley" described Twing emptying his sap buckets on Friday afternoon and turning them upside down until after sunset on Saturday so he would not profit from the sap that flowed from the trees on Sabbath.*

According to the Nearings, Twing was one of the best maple sugar makers in his neck of the woods and worked hard to have the first sugar to take to the Jamaica town meeting in March. A story that, according to the Nearings, was only a "tradition in the valley" described Twing emptying his sap buckets on Friday afternoon and turning them upside down until after sunset on Saturday so he would not profit from the sap that flowed from the trees on Sabbath.[37]

Irrespective of whether the story was true, it portrayed an image with which Twing was pleased. He could not have been happier that his neighbors recognized his conscientiousness and loyalty to his church. His commitment and Elizabeth's work both as a visiting nurse and an occasional literature salesperson left an imprint on their sons. Like many others in the rising generations of Jamaica's young, Joseph H. and James A. Twing foresaw their future unfolding in places other than their rural hometown. Both migrated south to the Seventh-day Adventist college town of South Lancaster, Massachusetts, for a college education. Joseph fulfilled a long career as a teacher and an ordained Seventh-day Adventist minister. James became a physician and a missionary. He was director of Heri Hospital in Tanzania, Africa, when he died at age fifty-one in a small plane mishap.[38]

Walter Twing never loosened his hold on a simple life, which was one of Jamaica's benchmarks. In June 1950, he punctuated the end of his active days by auctioning off his personal possessions. He had already sold his farm when the *Brattleboro Reformer* carried his announcement with a list of household goods—an old melodeon, a couple of desks, Boston rockers, stereoscopes, a candle mold, old wooden sugar buckets, farm tools, and other items that any antique dealer would have viewed opportunistically. "Terms cash," the announcement said with typical Green Mountain terseness.[39]

The Hurd Family

Also putting down deep roots in Pikes Falls were Floyd and Zoe Hurd. Floyd's Adventist heritage in Jamaica extended back through his mother, Lettie, to her parents, Charles M. and Clara E. Densmore. As converts from Isaac Sanborn's tent evangelism in Windham County during the summer of 1878, Floyd's grandparents had joined the Jamaica church on October 5 of that year.[40] Lettie married Massachusetts native George Hurd about 1895. Ten years later, the couple moved to the Stratton section of Pikes Falls.[41] George lost little time before injecting himself in civic affairs. In 1908, he became one of Stratton's selectmen, and in 1912, the town sent him to Montpelier as its representative in the state General Assembly.[42] He also served as a town road commissioner, a town lister, a member of the local grand jury, and leader of a school district.[43]

George and Lettie's son Floyd was sixteen years old when he married fifteen-year-old Zoe Linscott in 1914. From 1916 through 1940 the pair blessed the community with fifteen children. Floyd buried two of them under a tree on their farm. One had lived only a few hours after birth, and the other was stillborn.[44] But Floyd and Zoe were toughened by the harsh living conditions in the Green Mountains, and they hung on. They had also learned the responsibilities of citizenship when still young. At age twenty-four, Floyd followed his father to become Stratton's representative in the state House of Representatives. From 1934 through 1940 he was a selectman for Stratton, and for two years, 1933 and 1934, he held the office of town treasurer.[45]

During the 1930s, the life of the Hurds intersected with Helen and Scott Nearing. Scott Nearing was a former university professor who sharply disagreed with what he termed capitalist greed. The Nearings authored several books expanding on the virtues of the "good life," which in their opinion meant scorning comforts that could be construed as luxuries and subsisting off the land. Whenever the opportunity arose, they expressed their opposition to the "theories of a competitive, acquisitive, aggressive, war-making social order, which butchers for food and murders for sport and power."[46] The Nearings promoted ideas of community cooperation in contradiction to rugged and competitive individualism as a lifestyle.

These activities earned Scott Nearing and his wife a dubious reputation of being socialists, if not communists. Before the Nearings moved from Vermont in 1952, the House Un-American Activities Committee named Scott more than fifty times as a communist sympathizer. The Nearings had their strong opinions, but their experience in Pikes Falls did not mark them as Bolshevik revolutionaries. Despite their social and political baggage, much of their reputation was still a thing of the future when they moved into Pikes Falls in 1932, near the foot of Stratton Mountain.[47]

Floyd and Zoe Hurd lived about a quarter of a mile from Helen and Scott. If the Nearings' reputation frightened the Hurds, they did not let it show. Elizabeth Hurd Greene remembered that the Nearings were socialists but they never "tried to push their ideas on us."[48] The truth was that Helen and Scott were unprepared for their new life in Pikes Falls and needed all the help they could find to survive. Cooperation without agitation was a necessity for them. In 1936, Helen organized an Easter party and invited the community children. At least eight of the Hurd children went, the older ones carrying their toddling siblings in their arms.[49]

The Nearings credited the Hurds with teaching them how to produce maple syrup and sugar. During the first sugaring season after their arrival, Helen and Scott mistook the cloud of steam billowing out of the Hurds' sugarhouse for smoke. Hurrying to help extinguish the supposed flames, they found one of the Hurd girls operating the evaporator, which was boiling off water from the maple sap and producing the steam. What followed was the Nearings' first lesson, taught by a Pikes Falls teenager, about how to produce maple syrup.[50]

The Nearings saw this industry as a new possibility for living off the land while adding to their cash income at the same time, an idea more in keeping with survival in a capitalist environment than conformity to socialist thought. From 1933 to 1940 the Hurds and Nearings sugared together. Ignoring that this was a case of capitalist opportunism, in 1935 Helen made their association legal by signing a partnership agreement with Floyd to operate a maple sugar orchard. Hurd would take two-thirds of the syrup and Helen one-third. The orchard had 3,000 taps.[51]

But the Hurds were faithful members of the Pikes Falls church, and not much time elapsed before the question of Sabbath observance arose. Unlike Walter Twing, the Nearings said, Floyd Hurd emptied the sap buckets on Saturday, regarding it as an urgent chore, like milking the cows. Later, the conscience-smitten Hurds changed their minds and decided to leave the buckets unattended while they observed the Sabbath in a more strict manner. But the Nearings recalled that on several weekends the sap "ran like mad" and overflowed the buckets. While the Hurds were in church, Helen and Scott gathered the sap anyway and boiled it down to syrup.

"Then came the crucial question," the Nearings said. "Did the Hurds want to take their share of the syrup which had been made on the Sabbath, from sap that had run and been gathered that day?" Despite their change of heart, Floyd and Zoe Hurd were not Walter Twing. They debated the matter "earnestly," and in the end, they took their syrup.[52]

The Hurds may have taught the Nearings how to make syrup, but perhaps Floyd also felt their affirming attitudes as he priced farm products at bargain rates to cultivate a satisfied clientele. Helen and Scott said that anything they sold, including maple syrup, carried a price "not in terms of what the traffic would bear but in terms of the costs—figuring in our own time at going day wages."[53] In 1929, the spring before the Great Depression began, Hurd advertised in the *Atlantic Union Gleaner*, offering fancy-grade maple syrup to fellow church members for $2 a gallon. Ten years later he was still advertising for the same price, even though the average price for a gallon of fancy syrup was $3 at the time, the Nearings said.[54] No one could accuse Hurd of gouging his customers. Scott and Helen could applaud Floyd's practice as a virtue and an exemplary lack of greed.

By 1940, Floyd was looking for help to keep his farm going.[55] Elizabeth Hurd Greene, Floyd and Zoe's seventh child, recalled that it was about that time the family decided to move.[56] In 1941, they pulled up their stakes in Pikes Falls and resettled in Jericho near Essex Junction in the northern part of the state. Clara Densmore, who had been a member of the Jamaica church for more than sixty-two years, was also a part of the Hurd household at the time. Shortly, she passed away, one month short of her ninety-ninth birthday.[57] But the Hurds' house in Pikes Falls did not sell quickly. They had little recourse but to return to their old haunts in southern Vermont before finally selling out and making a clean break, moving to Heath, Massachusetts.[58]

The Dompier Family

Most of those whom we can identify as members of the Pikes Falls church bore Anglo-Saxon names and traced their ancestry through other locations in New England that were peopled by English-speaking settlers. In contrast was Joseph Dompier, a French-Canadian whose circuitous journey to Pikes Falls was typical of many immigrants from Quebec in search for a new life in the United States.

Joseph Dompier's ancestral line took him back to Charles Dompierre, a recruit in the Carignan Regiment that King Louis XIV dispatched to Nouvelle France in 1665 to protect French settlers from Indian attacks. After his military tour had ended, Charles settled on the Île d'Orléans, an island in the Saint Lawrence River immediately downstream from the provincial capital. His bride, Agnes Destouches, was one of the more than

700 *filles du roi* (Daughters of the King) responding to the king's call to migrate to Nouvelle France to become wives of soldiers who remained there after leaving the military.[59]

After wandering south to Terrebonne, about twenty-five miles north of Montreal, fourth-generation François Dompierre established a new line of the family in the adjacent town of Mascouche. At least five of his grandsons crossed the line into Vermont, probably during the 1850s as part of the migratory wave from Canada East to the United States. Among them was Joseph Dompierre who eventually found himself in Roxbury, a rural community in the central part of the state. In 1859, he married Alzina Cram, whose two older brothers, Emery P. and Loren D., were among the Sabbatarians who began observing the Saturday Sabbath shortly before the Seventh-day Adventist denomination was organized.[60]

Joseph and Alzina Dompier (the anglicized spelling dropped the final two letters of Joseph's name) remained in the Roxbury-Brookfield-Randolph area until 1870. Both A. C. Bourdeau and A. S. Hutchins visited their home as well as the homes of Alzina's brothers.[61] On a Saturday in August 1868, during one of his pastoral calls to the Dompiers, Bourdeau conducted an entire church service.

Credit: by the author

The family of Joseph Dompier (1834-1877), a French-Canadian immigrant, who moved to Pikes Falls from the Roxbury region of central Vermont in 1870.
Seated: left, Alzina Cram Dompier (1834-1899), wife of Joseph, and right, daughter, Irene (1860-1917). Standing: left to right, daughter Abbie (1870-1940), son Walter (1865-1938), and daughter, Eunice (1861-1928). The family moved back to central Vermont after Joseph died in Pikes Falls, 1877. Approximate date of picture, 1890.

Bourdeau and Joseph Dompier had much in common. Both were approximately the same age; at the time of their visit in 1868 they were thirty-three and thirty-four, respectively. Both were French-Canadians from the general region of Montreal, although Bourdeau had moved to Vermont in infancy, while Dompier had moved when an adult. Both were converts to Seventh-day Adventism, Bourdeau, a former Baptist, and Dompier, previously a French Catholic.

When Bourdeau visited the Dompiers in 1868, less than two months had passed since he had spent a week in Jamaica, framing the new meetinghouse and baptizing new members. At the time, the Jamaica congregation numbered more than thirty, a larger congregation than the company to which the Dompiers and Joseph's Cram in-laws belonged. Bourdeau's enthusiasm for the Jamaica church was evident in his official reports. It is not likely that he kept his compatriot in the dark about happenings at the meetinghouse in southern Vermont and that farmland in Windham County was cheap.

Two years after Bourdeau's visit with the Dompiers, Joseph and Alzina moved to Jamaica. We do not know their motivations. Of interest was the fact that Joseph's older brother, Louis, living in Brookfield, adjacent to both Roxbury and Randolph, had recently lost his wife and remarried. He drifted south into Windham County, but whether before or after Joseph and Alzina moved to Jamaica is not known.[62] Whatever the influence by Bourdeau and possibly Louis Dompier may have been, the Jamaica town records tell us that in November 1870, Joseph and Alzina bought a farm a short distance from the meetinghouse in Pikes Falls.[63]

At the time of their move, Joseph and Alzina were parents of four children, Irene, Eunice, Walter, and Abbie, aged ten years to eight months. We can only speculate that the family encountered financial difficulties in Jamaica. Before the move, Joseph had subscribed to the *Review* and contributed to various fundraising campaigns that the denomination sponsored, but those expenditures and donations appear to have slackened after he moved to Pikes Falls.[64] Not yet a full year elapsed when Joseph and Alzina sold their newly acquired property in November 1871.[65] But Joseph also renewed his reading. The *Review and Herald* noted in October 1876, that he paid for a subscription that would bring him the paper to April 1877.[66]

Joseph Dompier was battling more than bleak financial circumstances. On October 12, 1877, he died of tuberculosis, another victim of the scourge that had already claimed many lives in Pikes Falls. Loren, his brother-in-law, wrote that since converting to Seventh-day Adventism he "endeavored to live a consistent Christian life."[67]

Very little is known about the experience of the Dompiers in Pikes Falls. Their names do not appear in any of the reports that ministers filed after visiting the Jamaica church, and the family has no stories about their venture in southern Vermont. It is apparent that after the sale of their property, they continued to live and farm in Jamaica. The town records list Joseph as a farmer at the time of his death. In 1945, a Norman and Winifred Williams, newly arrived from Ohio, built a stone home over the old Dompier cellar hole. The farmhouse had long since disintegrated.[68] Without family ties or other connections to Jamaica, Alzina, forty-three years old and widowed, had no reason to stay. She and her four children returned to central Vermont, where they remained.

Joseph Dompier's grave marker stands in the tiny Pikes Falls Cemetery with those of about one dozen others, including Isaac and Jane Pike, and their son Henry. Only a few feet from the Pikes lie the remains of Marietta Bourn. Other Bourns and Wilders are buried in irregular rows. Trees have long since grown up and obscured their resting place, which, like their story, becomes visible only to those who search for it.

Trees have long since grown up and obscured their resting place, which, like their story, becomes visible only to those who search for it.

Notes

1. Young, *Echoes*, pp. 525, 526; "The Cause in Jamaica, Vt.," *RH*, November 17, 1868.
2. Ibid.
3. Bourdeau mentioned the depressed farm prices when discussing the Whites' move to Jamaica. Ibid. See also Young, *History*, p. 384, and Young, *Echoes*, pp. 525, 526; and Mark Worthen, *Hometown Jamaica*, p. 55.
4. "The Cause in Jamaica, Vt.," *RH*, November 17, 1868; "History of the Pikes Falls Church." Also, see William White's obituary, *RH*, September 30, 1890.

5. "Report from A. C. Bourdeau," *RH*, August 18, 1868. At the time of their move, the Whites had four children. The 1860 US Census lists six children of William and Melissa White, including what appear to be two sets of twins: Cassius, 15; Leslie, 14; Lester, 12; Chester, 12; Josephus, 4; Philinda, 4. Josephus was the middle name of Flavius. The 1870 Census includes neither Chester nor Philinda. Apparently one twin from each set did not reach adulthood.
6. "History of the Pike's Falls Church." According to the US Census, Flavius White was about thirteen years old in 1869.
7. Pike Diary, June 18, June 23, and August 22, 1869.
8. Young, *Echoes*, p. 526.
9. Worthen, *Hometown Jamaica*, pp. 42, 44; *Annual Report of the Commissioner of Patents for the Year 1891* (Washington, D.C.: 1892), pp. 392, 614; patent no. 525,803, issued September 11, 1894, United States Patent Office.
10. "Items of Interest," *Gleaner*, November 23, 1904.
11. Worthen, *Hometown Jamaica*, pp. 40–52.
12. "Obituary Notices," *Gleaner*, August 23, 1905.
13. "Vermont Conference Proceedings," *RH*, October 6, 1885.
14. "Vermont Conference Proceedings," *RH*, October 11, 1887.
15. "Vermont Conference Proceedings," *RH*, November 1, 1892.
16. "Vermont Conference Proceedings," *RH*, October 1, 1901.
17. Julius White, 1880 US Census Records.
18. "Vermont Conference Proceedings," *RH*, October 1, 1901.
19. "Rutland, Vt.," *Gleaner*, July 23, 1902; "Directory, Atlantic Union Conference," ibid.
20. "Report of the Vermont Conference," *Gleaner*, September 24, 1902.
21. "Items of Interest," Gleaner, November 23, 1904.
22. Worthen, *Hometown Jamaica*, pp. 42, 44; see the *Evening Recorder* (Amsterdam, New York), September 16, 1963.
23. "In Remembrance," *RH*, April 28, 1955.
24. 1880 US Census.
25. Ibid.; also see "Items of Interest," *Gleaner*, July 22, 1903.
26. 1880 US Census; "Obituary Notices," *Gleaner*, August 23, 1905. See "Items of Interest," *Gleaner*, November 23, 1904.
27. "Obituary Notices," *RH*, September 30, 1890.
28. *RH*, June 28, 1892.
29. "Obituaries," *RH*, October 16, 1900.
30. "Obituaries," *RH*, January 28, 1902.

31. To trace the movements of the Twing family, I have depended on US Census records, news articles, and obituaries. See "The New England Conference," *RH*, September 16, 1875; "Items of Interest," *Gleaner*, February 25, 1905; "Fund for the New England Sanitarium," *Gleaner*, September 6, 1905; and "Obituary Notices," *Gleaner*, April 18, 1934.
32. "Fund for the New England Sanitarium," *Gleaner*, September 6, 1905.
33. Young, *Echoes*, p. 498; handwritten note on local map supplied by the Jamaica town clerk, 2007; "No. New England: Church Directory," *Gleaner*, December 4, 1912.
34. See "No. New England," *Gleaner*, October 14, 1914, for a statement about one of Twing's contacts with Mason S. Stone, State Superintendent of Education. Giving to Twing became an annual ritual for Stone even after he became lieutenant governor of the state. "Visiting the People," *Gleaner*, December 13, 1922.
35. See photograph of the Walter Twing family in Worthen, *Hometown Jamaica*, p. 127. Walter Twing's sales reports appeared frequently in the *Gleaner*, beginning in the March 4, 1914, issue. The *Gleaner* published his last report in the December 20, 1946, issue.
36. "A Twelve-Thousand-Dollar Institute," *Gleaner*, February 16, 1916.
37. Nearing, *Good Life*, pp. 172, 173.
38. "At Rest," *RH*, May 22, 1997; "In Brief," *RH*, February 24, 1972; "Medical Director Urgently Needed," *RH*, March 23, 1972.
39. *Brattleboro Reformer*, June 12, 1950, cited in Joly, *Almost Utopia*, p. 30.
40. "Obituary Notices," *Gleaner*, February 2, 1941. The obituary mistakenly attributes the tent evangelistic meetings to "Elders Stone and Butler," but Isaac Sanborn documented his tent meetings in *RH* during the summer of 1878. He specifically mentioned the baptism on October 5, 1878, in Jamaica when the obituary states that Densmores joined the Jamaica church. See "Vermont," *RH*, October 24, 1878.
41. Young, *Echoes*, p. 243.
42. Town Records of Stratton, Vermont, Book 2, pp. 469, 505.
43. Ibid., pp. 478–480.
44. Young, *Echoes*, p. 246; Young, *History*, p. 434.
45. Young, *Echoes*, p. 244; Young, *History*, pp. 140, 142; Auditor's Report, 1921, Stratton Town Records. Email, D. K, Young to Floyd Greenleaf, August 23, 2012.
46. Nearing, *Good Life*, pp. 194, 195.
47. Ibid., p. 17. Also see Jean Hay Bright, *Meanwhile, Next Door to the Good Life* (Dixmont, ME; BrightBerry Press, 2003) for a commentary on the Nearings' good life.

48. Telephone interview, Floyd Greenleaf with Elizabeth Hurd Greene, October 1, 2012.
49. Young, *Echoes*, p. 245.
50. Elizabeth Hurd Greene, telephone interview by Floyd Greenleaf, October 1, 2012.
51. Young, *Echoes*, p. 244. See Helen and Scott Nearing, *The Maple Sugar Book*, 50th anniversary edition (White River Junction, VT: Chelsea Green Publishing Company, 2000), p. 271. Also, see information on page 172.
52. Nearing, *Good Life*, p. 173.
53. Ibid., p. 33.
54. See Hurd's advertisements in *Gleaner*, Apr. 3, 1929 and Apr. 12, 1939. For the price of maple syrup in 1940 see Nearing, *Maple Sugar*, p. 273.
55. *Gleaner*, March 20, 1940.
56. Elizabeth Greene, telephone interviews by Floyd Greenleaf, December 5, 2007, and May 6, 2012.
57. "Obituary Notices," *Gleaner*, February 26, 1941.
58. Young, *Echoes*, p. 244; "Obituary Notices," *Gleaner*, February 2, 1941. See also Young, *History*, p. 393.
59. The number of women included in the *filles du roi* varies with different accounts, sometimes exceeding 1000. I have used the website, http://1ref.us/hg, for a compilation of the members of the Carignan Regiment and Daughters of the King (filles du roi) as found in René Jetté, *Dictionnaire Généologique des Familles du Québec* (Montreal: Les Presses de l'Université de Montreal, 1983). Accessed on August 21, 2012.
60. For the details of the Dompierre/Dompier family, see Jetté, *Dictionnaire*; Cyprien Tanguay, *Dictionnaire Généologique des Familles Canadiennes* (Québec: Eusèbe Senécal, 1871–1890); Lucien Rivest, *Mariages du Comté de l'Assomption* (Montreal: Quintin Publications, 1972); *St-Henri de Mascouche, Comté de L'Assomption, 1750–1993* (Joliette, Québec: Société de généalogie de Lanaudière, 2000); parish records in Les Archives Nationales du Québec; and Vermont Vital Records, Middlesex, Vermont.
61. "Report from A. C. Bourdeau," *RH*, October 6, 1868; "Report from Bro. Hutchins," *RH*, March 30, 1869.
62. Vermont Vital Records. Louis Dompier became a section boss for the Brattleboro and Windsor Railroad. His son, John, also worked for the railroad (*Gazetteer*, pp. 437, 489).
63. Jamaica Town Records.

64. See business report section of *RH*, June 2, 1863, March 22, 1864, May 15, 1866, October 20, 1868, August 31, 1869, November 22, 1870.
65. Jamaica Town Records.
66. "Receipts for *Review and Herald*," *RH*, October 19, 1876.
67. "Obituary Notices," *RH*, January 17, 1878.
68. *Vermont Phoenix*, July 20, 1945, cited in Joly, *Almost Utopia*, p. 57.

Decline and Demise

With a brief notice in small print on the next-to-the-last page of the *Review,* William Covert announced that Jamaica would be the site of a general meeting of Seventh-day Adventists in Vermont, scheduled for the extended weekend of February 14–17, 1896. Suggesting that a "large number should be present," Covert confirmed that R. C. Porter, the superintendent of the district, would attend. "Come, all who can," Covert urged.[1]

The "district" that Covert referred to was District 1, a region that included conferences of churches in New England, New York, New Jersey, Pennsylvania, Maryland, Virginia, and West Virginia. However, this meeting was exclusively for the Vermont Conference. Covert did not explain the reason for an unusual conference-wide meeting in the dead of a Green Mountain winter or why it was to convene at Jamaica, a place that from the vantage point of transportation and communication was an out-of-the-way location. If the conference president wanted to encourage a large number of Vermonters, statewide, to hazard winter travel, he could have better selected a location in the northwestern part of the state, where the Adventist population was more concentrated and members would not have to venture as far as Jamaica.

Covert had already told Porter that he wanted to transfer out of Vermont because of the hard winters.[2] In January 1893, he had postponed baptisms in Jamaica because ice covered the small river that flowed by the meetinghouse.[3] If he chose Jamaica as the location for the meetings, perhaps he remembered that event and thought that the largest church in Vermont would lend itself best to underscoring his complaint about the winters in the Green Mountains.

But Porter may have chosen the location for the meetings. Since 1891, he had been a conference president in New England and knew the challenges of Vermont winters. He had only recently become superintendent of District 1. We are left to guess that quite simply, he was making dutiful rounds of his territory after assuming new responsibilities and regarded a gathering in Jamaica as an opportunity to introduce himself to Vermont Adventists. But we are only speculating. Regardless of the possible reasons why Jamaica had become the venue for the meeting, it was a gesture that recognized this congregation's prominent place in the Vermont Conference.

Jamaica's importance to Sabbatarianism began when Joseph Bates visited the community in 1853 to follow up an earlier visit by fellow ministers Wheeler and Day. As one of the founders of the Seventh-day Adventist Church, Bates was on a mission to spread Sabbatarian beliefs in new territory.

That Bates reported his experience in the Sabbatarian press was not surprising. Sabbatarian ministers commonly communicated to the public in this manner. His meeting with a handful of discouraged former Millerites in Jamaica appeared in the *Review* at a time when Sabbatarians were few but eager for the companionship that their common experiences, shared in the press, would bring them.

Similarly, because Seventh-day Adventists did not own many church buildings in the 1860s, a sequence of stories about a new meetinghouse in Pikes Falls was news of denominational interest. Although the Jamaica church was not a leading denominational congregation, it was an important congregation in Vermont and northern New England. It both represented and fostered the progress of the Seventh-day Adventist Church, not merely in the surrounding community, but in entire southern Vermont.

Signs of Decline

The first straw in the wind that presaged the decline of the Jamaica church was the fact that the *Review* did not carry a report of the meeting that Covert announced. Church leaders typically followed such meetings with an article in the *Review* that described the gathering to assure the Adventist world that all was well in their field. That no report appeared was a possible sign that nothing noteworthy occurred.

Doubtless, no one sensed at the time that the Jamaica church would soon begin its decline and eventually die. We cannot pinpoint when the slump set in, but we can infer that infrequent and less significant news about Jamaica after this moment in 1896 suggests that the congregation played a lessening role in conference affairs.

However, at least in part, Jamaica's sparse appearances in the Adventist press after the mid-1890s was the result of organizational change within the denomination. By 1898, the total Seventh-day Adventist membership was nearly 60,000, of whom more than 10,000 lived in missions that circled the earth.[4] Local congregations remained the basic entity in church affairs, but a growing world organization progressively placed more emphasis on health-care centers, schools, and publishing houses. Consequently, editors of the *Review* gave priority to news of universal church interest—world missions and institutions—and less attention to individual congregations. Although the Pikes Falls church had carved out its prominent niche in Vermont's Adventist community by the 1890s, its proportional importance in the world organization was diminishing.

After the turn of the century, the responsibility for local church news shifted from the *Review* to papers published by the newly organized unions that replaced the former districts. Unions were regional clusters of conferences with a complete set of elected officers rather than a single appointed leader, such as R. C. Porter. The creation of unions began in 1901, and almost immediately they started to publish their own papers for their constituencies. The Vermont Conference was part of the newly organized Atlantic Union, which, beginning in 1902, produced the *Atlantic Union Gleaner*, commonly shortened to the *Gleaner*, that carried news from individual churches in the union.

In 1910, the Vermont Conference merged with New Hampshire to form the Northern New England Conference, and in 1923 this entity added Maine. The Pikes Falls congregation lost traction not only because it was less conspicuous in a growing world organization but also because it found itself part of an enlarging entity in which other churches were more visible.

Because records for the Pikes Falls church are not extant, and nineteenth-century members are no longer available for interviews, the *Gleaner* has become the recognized source of information about the congregation.

Most of the news that this paper carried about Vermont Adventists originated in churches in the northern part of the state; stories about Pikes Falls appeared in the *Gleaner* only occasionally, often as a perfunctory tidbit. Typical of all church publications, the *Gleaner* thrived on reports of progress and did not often discuss decline, but scant mention of Jamaica in its columns was symptomatic of the congregation's regression.

A possible omen of decline in the Pikes Falls church showed up in the tithe reports that the conference treasurer published. An up-and-down pattern of tithe remissions from the churches to the conference was common in Vermont, indicating that payments by individual members were irregular. Notwithstanding this caveat, figures from Jamaica were not consistently larger than those from other congregations, even though its membership was much larger.[5]

It is possible that some members in Jamaica may not have paid tithe, which resulted in a lower rank in the list of churches than might be expected,[6] but the logical inference of the reports is that the Jamaica congregation as a body earned less income than members elsewhere in the state. These financial reports confirmed what earlier visiting ministers had observed: the Jamaica church was not financially well off.

Members demonstrated they would empty their purses when circumstances appealed to them to respond to church needs.

But financial news from Pikes Falls was mixed. Members demonstrated they would empty their purses when circumstances appealed to them to respond to church needs. In 1904, a drive for funds to help move the denominational headquarters from Battle Creek, Michigan, to Washington, D.C., led the Pikes Falls members to circulate a spontaneous pledge form that raised what the conference president called "liberal" amounts. Five years later, after denominational leaders inaugurated a plan to raise funds for world missions, the Jamaica congregation pledged the second-highest amount in Vermont.[7] In 1912, after the Vermont Conference merged with New Hampshire, Jamaica remitted the fourth-highest amount of tithe among the thirty congregations in the Northern New England Conference; the following year Jamaica ranked sixth.[8]

Brief Revival Under O. O. and Carrie Farnsworth

The scarcity of news from Jamaica did not mean that conference leaders had abandoned the congregation. A conference representative conducted a conference in the Pikes Falls church in August 1903, to encourage wider and better participation in Sabbath schools. Various members prepared papers that they read to stimulate discussion.[9]

Prospects seemed to brighten in 1908 when O. O. Farnsworth settled in Jamaica as the pastor with duties extending to southern Vermont.[10] Since 1905, he had served as president of the Vermont Conference.[11] His outgoing manner grabbed the attention of Methodists in nearby Bondville, who requested him to serve as their interim pastor while their presiding elder looked for a replacement.

Farnsworth could not refuse this unusual gesture of Christian brotherhood. To his Methodist church he presented the commonalities of Christian beliefs that bridged denominational differences, but he also unabashedly preached sermons with Adventist content. Members of his Sunday congregation said that they listened to sermons such as they had never heard before. Seven months later a permanent minister arrived to end Farnsworth's unconventional pastorate, but not before one member switched membership from the Bondville Methodist Church to the Pikes Falls Seventh-day Adventist Church.[12]

Farnsworth's reputation as a pastor-for-hire followed him to the Congregational church in Jamaica, where he began another temporary pastorate in the fall of 1911.[13] With claims that his discourses on the sanctuary and other biblical topics that had a specific Adventist twist broke down prejudice and inspired appreciation among his Sunday-keeping neighbors, Farnsworth also won the approbation of his own conference president.

Farnsworth's time spent with the Bondville Methodists and the Jamaica Congregationalists did not require him to neglect his own Seventh-day Adventist flock. As winter began in late 1910, he conducted a week of prayer and spiritual emphasis in the Pikes Falls church. "Storm and cold" prevented some of the meetings, he wrote, but he doggedly kept on, presenting the already prepared readings and otherwise encouraging the faithful. At the end of the week, a thankful congregation donated a larger offering than the church had garnered in years.[14]

With the help of his wife, Carrie, Farnsworth revived the elementary school that had been defunct for about twenty-five years. Carrie had taught school before moving to Jamaica, but she was better known as an organist and a Bible worker. In Pikes Falls she became the first teacher of the reestablished school in 1908.[15] It was enough to inspire the church to continue the school until 1917. Following Carrie Farnsworth was Lillian Kelsey, an experienced teacher among Adventists in northern New England, who taught in Jamaica from 1909 to 1911.

In 1910, the school moved from the church to a separate building, "nestled among the green hills," Kelsey wrote, and enrollment rose to sixteen, the largest number in the history of the church. In keeping with Farnsworth's successful outreach to Christians of other faiths, some of the students were from non-Adventist homes and, with their parents, were attending the Pikes Falls church.[16] Eva B. Abbott, C. H. Linscott, Mattie B. Tefft, Lena Taylor, and Muriel Wyman succeeded Lillian Kelsey as teachers.[17]

Farnsworth remained in Jamaica about five years. In 1913, church employment took him to Canada. Once again, the Pikes Falls congregation and southern Vermont were without a minister. The school continued until 1917, and at least for a time, some non-Adventist students attended.[18] The church reestablished the school in 1924,[19] but it was a short-lived venture. Again, in 1929, Elizabeth Twing began a seven-year stint as a church school teacher. The *Gleaner* carried no information about reopening the church school in Pikes Falls, which suggests that Elizabeth Twing may have conducted a home school for her three sons, Joseph, William, and James. It was possible that others attended, but immediately after Elizabeth ended her teaching, all three Twing boys were enrolled in South Lancaster Academy in Massachusetts.[20]

Membership Losses and Demise

As competent as they were, the efforts of the Farnsworths and the teachers in the church school did not stop the Pikes Falls congregation from its free fall. The key issue was a loss of members. No one knows how long the membership list became after it reached ninety-nine members in October 1893. When planning a reunion weekend for the Pikes Falls church in 1939, the pastor for the region reported that he had been told the membership had once been 150. Later, a different district pastor placed the figure at 125.[21] No substantiation exists for either figure.

During his tour of Vermont early in 1904, F. M. Dana, the conference secretary and treasurer, visited the Jamaica congregation, which he described as one of the "larger companies."[22] In contrast, however, after a visit to the church in February 1905, J. W. Watt, the conference president, commented that the "Jamaica church has been greatly reduced in membership by removals, but the few who remain are of good courage and are faithful in the work of the Lord."²³ It is not clear if Watt was referring to the loss of members resulting from the transfer of White Mop Wringer Company out of Jamaica or to a general loss of members, but 1905 was the year that J. G. and Hubert White closed their mop wringer shop and took a group of employees and family members with them to resume operations in New York. If decline had set in by 1905, we can conclude that membership peaked at some point during the twelve years between 1893 and 1905.

For the congregation that had become the largest Seventh-day Adventist Church in Vermont and, in all probability, in the three states of northern New England, the membership drain was painful. In 1917, the Sabbath school in Pikes Falls reported only twenty-six members, placing eighth on a list of Sabbath schools in Vermont and New Hampshire. Two years later, this number slipped to seventeen members, or fourteenth among twenty-eight churches in the conference.²⁴

Other signs pointed to downward-spiraling membership. Some families sold their holdings and moved away. A. C. Stevens, a prominent member of the church, advertised two farms for sale in September 1911. Six months later Calvin Pike, one of the charter members of the church, put his farm on the market. In less than two months, O. O. Farnsworth announced another farm for sale, presumably his own.²⁵ After sitting through a rousing set of meetings in 1917, a couple pledged their farm of eighty-five acres to support denominational projects.²⁶ Similarly convicted in 1923, another family deeded their forty acres of pasture and timber to the Northern New England Conference to be sold to benefit missions.²⁷ During the spring and summer of 1925, the *Gleaner* carried simultaneous advertisements of three farms that Adventist owners wished to sell.²⁸

The exodus of members struck a telling blow to the church and its activities.

The exodus of members struck a telling blow to the church and its activities. Elizabeth Hurd Greene, who attended the church in the late 1920s and 1930s, recalls little activity in the congregation. A decline in membership that began before her time continued until there was "not much of a church service," if any at all, she remembers.²⁹

Greene recalls that her family attended the Sabbath school in Pikes Falls each Saturday morning but went to West Townshend for the preaching. Within a year or so after the dedication of a new Townshend church in 1936,[30] the Hurds skipped the Pikes Falls church altogether in order to worship in West Townshend. It is likely that they were not the only ones. Howard Hurd, Elizabeth's younger brother, recollects nothing specific about worshipping at Pikes Falls, but he knows that services occurred because he remembers the church members' horses in the church sheds.[31]

Beginning in 1919, the Northern New England Conference officers divided their territory into pastoral districts that included multiple congregations, sometimes separated by fifty miles or more. To shepherd these flocks, assigned pastors lived near the largest church and scheduled their trips to outlying congregations. Forming pastoral districts proved to be a continuing practice, but depending on changes within the churches, district lines could also change.

The decline of the Pikes Falls church was obvious in 1937 when Carroll Pike, a great-grandson of Isaac Newton Pike, became pastor of the district that included Pikes Falls, his ancestral congregation, while he lived about forty miles away in White River Junction, a small city on the Vermont bank of the Connecticut River.[32] In 1940, after he transferred to Massachusetts, his younger brother, Victor, followed him as district pastor.[33]

Two years later, in 1942, when conference leaders carved out a new pastoral district in southern Vermont that revolved around Brattleboro, all doubt vanished that the center of church gravity in southern Vermont had shifted away from Jamaica. Besides Brattleboro, the new district included the Pikes Falls church and congregations in West Townshend and Bennington.[34] That Brattleboro was the prominent church in southern Vermont was even more apparent the next year when it hosted an all-day gathering of church officers from Jamaica and other churches in the region.[35]

The last allusion the *Gleaner* carried about an organized congregation in Jamaica appeared in 1945. At that time, the news article declared, the Sabbath school in Jamaica was functioning well, following the example of other large churches in the Northern New England Conference. The next year the district pastor referred to Walter and Elizabeth Twing as the "only two remaining members" of the Pikes Falls congregation.[36]

Jamaica's Legacy

During the years of decline, the noteworthy church events in Pikes Falls were regional meetings. As the mother congregation of Adventists in southern Vermont, this church had often been the gathering place for general meetings. After decline set in, these meetings drew attention to the spiritual value of preserving an artifact of denominational history. Following a set of meetings in 1931, F. D. Wells, president of the Northern New England Conference, assured readers of the *Gleaner* that the "Spirit of God came very near to us as we sang and prayed and studied the Bible together in this old church that has been used so many years by our people."[37]

Ten years later conference leaders encouraged southern Vermonters to attend the annual regional services in Pikes Falls, announcing that "it is a real inspiration to meet in these old landmarks."[38] A. F. Ruf, who was in charge of Sabbath schools, education, and missionary activities in the Northern New England Conference, alluded to the meetinghouse when he remarked in 1943 that the regional meetings were "always held in Pikes Falls."[39]

Members in the area who recalled their childhood attendance in the old meetinghouse organized a reunion in September 1939,[40] to celebrate the history and legacy of the Pikes Falls congregation. In 1942, a repeat of this event brought D. A. Ochs, president of the Northern New England Conference, to Pikes Falls to draw inspiration from the church's past.

Credit: Photo by the author
The Seventh-day Adventist meetinghouse in Pikes Falls, remodeled into a private home, as seen in 2012.

To prepare for the meeting, members from West Townshend and Brattleboro gave the Jamaica meetinghouse a new coat of paint, which hints that the membership in Jamaica was not substantial enough to undertake the project. Visitors flocked to Pikes Falls from all over southern Vermont—Brattleboro and Bennington as well as nearby communities. They brought their lunches and picnicked on the church grounds between the morning and afternoon meetings.

As a newcomer to the Northern New England Conference, Ochs had probably never been to Jamaica, but his visit swept him away with emotion and nostalgia. Memorabilia met him everywhere he looked in the church. Books and periodicals dating back ninety years to the Sabbatarian decade of the 1850s, and old second-advent songbooks and charts illustrating the Ten Commandments and biblical prophecies gave the sanctuary the aura of a museum. At the rear of the church, Ochs noted the folding doors that closed off a portion that had once been "occupied by a church school," he said. The "crude" desks and other school paraphernalia were still in place. The antiquated benches in the sanctuary, the platform "made of hundreds of square blocks of hardwood" (installed by Flavius White at the time of construction, 1868–71), the massive chandelier with oil lamps, and the two wood stoves with pipes extending the length of the sanctuary carried Ochs back to an era whose inspiration he did not want to forget.[41]

In 1946, the district pastor organized the annual regional meeting as a virtual journey backward through time, giving old members a chance to relive the days when the church was a monument to Adventism in southern Vermont. A member of the West Townshend congregation recounted the history of the Jamaica church, and an elderly granddaughter of Isaac and Jane Pike recalled her days as a student in the church school during the 1880s. Fittingly, R. W. Moore, the conference president, told the congregation that the conference would keep the old building permanently,[42] implying that it was no longer an active church.

A. E. Millner, conference president, explained in 1959 that scheduling the annual regional meetings at Pikes Falls was a deliberate plan "to keep close to the spirit of Adventism and to again recapture the zeal and ardor of our forefathers."[43] But Millner did not know that he was issuing the epitaph for the regional meetings in the historic Pikes Falls meetinghouse. Time had taken its toll. With deterioration setting in, the Pikes Falls church was undergoing repairs when conference leaders postponed the meeting the next year.[44]

By this time, pragmatism rather than nostalgic inspiration became the order of the day. The church had long since ceased to be a weekly gathering place for worshipers, and conference leaders realized that maintaining a building for infrequent use was no longer financially viable. In 1966, the conference sold the Pikes Falls meetinghouse,[45] four or five years short of the hundredth anniversary of its dedication as a new place of worship. Not included in the sale was the tiny cemetery on the knoll behind the church where some of the early members of the congregation had lain for nearly a century. With this transfer of ownership, one of the monuments of Seventh-day Adventist history in Vermont disappeared.

> *Not included in the sale was the tiny cemetery on the knoll behind the church where some of the early members of the congregation had lain for nearly a century.*

We can generalize that the demise of the Pikes Falls church resulted from a combination of causes, but more than anything else, Elizabeth Hurd Greene saw it very simply as a matter of members "dying off or moving away."[46] Historians may explain the church's demise however they will, but Greene's observation, as simplistic as it may sound, perhaps is as close to the truth as anything could be.

Notes

1. "Appointments," *RH*, January 28, 1896.
2. R. C. Porter had informed church leaders in Michigan about Covert's wishes. A month following the Vermont general meeting, Covert received his new assignment to be president of the Wisconsin Conference. How much better the winters in Wisconsin were than winters in Vermont is open to question. See Minutes, General Conference Committee, January 28, 1895, March 19, 1896.
3. "Vermont," *RH*, February 7, 1893.
4. *General Conference Bulletin*, 1899. The *Bulletin* was a day-to-day report of the sessions of the General Conference of Seventh-day Adventists that occurred each year through 1889. The frequency of the sessions later changed to two-year, four-year, and five-year intervals. Hereafter this source cited as *GC Bulletin*.
5. Systematic Benevolence, discussed earlier in this study, officially ceased in 1879 when Seventh-day Adventists adopted tithing and additional donations as a means of church support. Both tithing and other donations were voluntary; that is, they were not a test of membership,

110   *Nearly Forgotten*

but church leaders placed much importance on financial support by individual members.
6. The treasurer of the Vermont Conference published periodic tithe reports that named each church with the amount sent to the conference. See *Gleaner* for the years 1901–1909, *passim.*
7. "Vermont, Rutland, Manchester, Bennington, Jamaica," *Gleaner,* June 15, 1904; "Of Interest to Vermont Friends," *Gleaner,* October 6, 1909.
8. The conference treasurer reported church tithe for 1912 and 1913 in *Gleaner,* January 28, 1914.
9. "Sabbath-School Convention at Jamaica, Vt." *Gleaner,* September 9, 1903.
10. A news note in *Gleaner,* March 11, 1908, reads: "The permanent address of O. O. Farnsworth is Jamaica, Vt."
11. "Northern New England Conference," *SDA Encyclopedia,* 2nd rev. ed., vol. M–Z, p. 215.
12. "Vermont," *Gleaner,* October 27, 1909; *Gleaner,* "Bondville, Vt." May 11, 1910.
13. "Jamaica," *Gleaner,* April 5, 1911.
14. "The Week of Prayer in the Atlantic Union," *Gleaner,* January 4, 1911.
15. "Vermont," *Gleaner,* May 5, 1909. The *Yearbook,* 1909, lists Carrie Farnsworth as the church school teacher in Jamaica, which probably reflected her experience during the previous year. See also Carrie Farnsworth's obituary, *RH,* October 30, 1941, and the *Pacific Union Recorder,* September 24, 1941.
16. "Vermont," *Gleaner,* Oct. 27, 1909; "Closing Exercises of the Jamaica, Vermont, Church-School," *Gleaner,* July 13, 1910; "A Word from the Church-Schools of Northern New England," *Gleaner,* October 10, 1910; "Items," *Gleaner,* May 31, 1911.
17. *Yearbook,* 1909–1917.
18. "Jamaica Church-School," *Gleaner,* June 22, 1914.
19. "In Southern Vermont," *Gleaner,* August 6, 1924; "Our Schools," *Gleaner,* September 24, 1924.
20. See lists of church school teachers for the Northern New England Conference in *Yearbook,* 1929–1935. A news note in the *Gleaner,* April 6, 1936, p. 6, states that Mrs. Walter Twing was visiting her three sons in South Lancaster.
21. "Pikes Falls General Meeting," *Gleaner,* September 20, 1939; "Pikes Falls Meeting," *Gleaner,* October 4, 1946.
22. "Field Work in Vermont," *Gleaner,* March 2, 1904.

23. "Vermont, Windham, Jamaica, and Taftsville," *Gleaner*, February 22, 1905.
24. "Financial Report of the Sabbath-Schools, *Gleaner*, May 16, 1917; "Report of Sabbath-Schools," *Gleaner*, May 28, 1919.
25. See advertisements in *Gleaner*, September 20, 1911, March 20, 1912, and May 1, 1912.
26. "Closing the General Meetings," *Gleaner*, November 7, 1917.
27. Advertisement, *Gleaner*, July 25, 1923.
28. See *Gleaner*, April 8, April 22, and July 1.
29. Elizabeth Hurd Greene, telephone interview by Floyd Greenleaf, May 6, 2012.
30. "Dedication of Church, *Gleaner*, August 19, 1936.
31. Howard Hurd, telephone interview by Floyd Greenleaf, May 6, 2012.
32. An announcement in the *Gleaner*, March 31, 1937, stated that C. M. (Carroll) Pike's new address was White River Junction. He had moved from Maine where he had become an ordained minister.
33. As pastor of the district, V. R. (Victor) Pike announced an all-day meeting at Pikes Falls on September 14, 1940. *Gleaner*, September 4, 1940.
34. "Districts," *Gleaner*, July 8, 1942.
35. "Notices," *Gleaner*, March 24, 1943.
36. "Fine Example of Our Two Largest Churches," *Gleaner*, May 4, 1945; "Pikes Falls Meeting," *Gleaner*, October 4, 1946.
37. "General Meetings," *Gleaner*, July 29, 1931.
38. "News Notes," *Gleaner*, September 10, 1941.
39. "Meeting to be Held in Pikes Falls," *Gleaner*, September 8, 1943.
40. "Pikes Falls General Meeting," *Gleaner*, September 20, 1939.
41. "Brattleboro District," *Gleaner*, October 28, 1942; "Meeting at Pikes Falls Church," *Gleaner*, September 2, 1942; "An Old Landmark," *RH*, September 24, 1942.
42. "Pikes Falls Meeting," *Gleaner*, October 4, 1946.
43. "Important Gatherings," *Gleaner*, June 29, 1959.
44. "Postponement of Pikes Falls Meeting," *Gleaner*, July 18, 1960.
45. Book 36, Jamaica Town Records, pp. 291, 293.
46. Elizabeth Hurd Greene, telephone interview by Floyd Greenleaf, May 6, 2012.

Retrospect

The disappearance of the Pikes Falls church did not arouse discussion in the Adventist press. To propose a definitive explanation of the causes for the church's decline would be to attempt the impossible, but this chapter suggests some conditions associated with its demise.

Changes Within Adventism

When William Covert left the presidency of the Vermont Conference in 1896, conference finances were in reasonably good order. Prudent management of church resources enabled him to divert much conference energy to southern Vermont. However, with the nation reeling from the Panic of 1893, not much time elapsed after Covert's departure before the conference began to downsize. The southern Vermont camp meetings ceased, and the number of pastors diminished. Reduced resources led to less activity and fewer pastoral visits to Jamaica.

Discontinuity in church leadership became commonplace, not by design, but by default. During the fourteen years between 1896 and 1910, the Vermont Conference functioned under six different presidents. The number of ordained ministers sometimes dwindled to two, who also usually held conference administrative duties. The home addresses of all ministers reveal that they lived in the northern half of the state.[1] These circumstances resulted in a repeat of the pattern of pastoral oversight of earlier years: the majority of Adventists lived in the northern part of the state and received more attention than the minority who lived in southern Vermont. The net effect of this situation was to shunt the Jamaica church and southern Vermont again to the periphery of conference affairs. The Pikes Falls church was no stranger to these circumstances.

It is necessary to remember, however, that resident pastors were a blessing that Seventh-day Adventist churches in Vermont, and throughout North America for that matter, never routinely enjoyed until the third decade of the twentieth century. Typically, ministers lived near a church to which they gave their attention, but they did not limit themselves to a single congregation. The few who moved to Jamaica had always arrived with the understanding that they were regional pastors, not ministers for the Jamaica church exclusively. In that sense, the Jamaica church was not unlike the others.

But membership gains gave the Jamaica congregation hope for at least a permanent regional pastor. Despite its standing as the largest congregation in the conference, the church continued to fend for itself between visits that conference leaders and other pastors could squeeze into their schedules. When the conference president passed through Jamaica in 1904, he confessed it was his first visit in two years. The Pikes Falls church could not have expected much more. At the time, the conference could afford only two other ordained ministers and one licensed minister, who was also the conference secretary and treasurer.[2]

In 1910, Seventh-day Adventist churches in Vermont and New Hampshire merged to form the Northern New England Conference. Thirteen years later this entity expanded to include Maine. Perhaps financial issues contributed to this organizational change, although we cannot overlook improvements in travel and communication that made the administration of larger conferences easier as well as more cost-effective. One of the effects that Vermont Adventists felt from these mergers was to see their headquarters move from Vermont eventually to Portland, Maine.[3]

The mergers with New Hampshire and Maine did not bring pastors to Jamaica more frequently.[4] The distance from Bennington, Vermont, in the southwest corner of the Northern New England Conference to Presque Isle, Maine, in the northeast approximated 500 miles. To cover this territory, ministers were as scarce as when Vermont stood alone as a separate state conference. Even as late as 1930, only seven ministers, both ordained and licensed, in addition to conference leaders were available to serve the forty churches spread across the three states of northern New England.

Whatever negative impact these changes in the northern states of New England may have exerted on the Pikes Falls church, they do not explain the demise of the congregation, because to varying degrees, all churches felt the pinch of tight finances and the lack of pastors. Because the Jamaica church was large at the turn of the twentieth century, the odds against it seemed greater and its decline more conspicuous.

Of major significance is the fact that as much as the Northern New England Conference suffered from a lack of financial resources, decline in Jamaica ran contrary to the broader trend of denominational growth. Not only did the world church report annual increases in membership, but membership also expanded in the Northern New England Conference. In 1910, Seventh-day Adventist membership in Vermont, New Hampshire, and Maine (at the time, Maine was a separate conference) totaled 872, a figure that more than doubled by 1940 when it reached 1,862.[5] While the Jamaica congregation was declining, new Seventh-day Adventist churches in southern Vermont were organizing. These facts suggest that conditions peculiar to Jamaica significantly affected the church.

Demographic and Economic Changes Affecting the Church

Mark Worthen's bicentennial book, *Hometown Jamaica,* paints an appealing picture of a Vermont village that symbolized rural and homespun life, the stuff that has traditionally fed patriotism and makes Americans proud to be Americans. In the context of Paul Searls's analysis of Vermont history, Jamaica was a showcase of "uphill" values.

But as the nineteenth century closed and the twentieth began, economic decline became progressively apparent in Jamaica. A contributing factor was a loss of residents, which translated into a loss of markets and productivity. The ten-year enumerations of the United States Census reveal that the population of the Jamaica township peaked at more than 1,600 in 1850, immediately before the visits by Frederick Wheeler and Joseph Bates when they brought Sabbatarianism to the community. By 1900, the township population stood at only half of that number,[6] and for a half century beginning in 1920, the population fluctuated below 590, descending to its nadir of 496 in 1960.

In 1945, the United States Postal Service discontinued its rural mail delivery route to Pikes Falls, excusing itself by saying that the operation was too costly for only fourteen families who remained in the combined Stratton and Jamaica portions of the hamlet. Population loss was undeniable. In 1868, at least twenty families occupied this stretch of rural road.[7]

Despite the town's attractive hominess and down-to-earth air that Worthen describes, rising generations of Jamaicans had reasons for pessimism because of less promising economic conditions in their community. The town's primary challenge was how to maintain at least its *status quo* in the face of an eroding economy and a declining population.

It is not one of the purposes of this study to determine what caused the decline in Jamaica, but the general lines of the downturn are relevant if we are to understand the conditions that the Pikes Falls church faced. Population growth throughout the state slowed to a trickle during the last decades of the nineteenth century and through the first half of the twentieth, partially as a result of residents moving westward to more promising farmland. Lewis Stilwell believes that this migration began as early as 1795, long before Vermont was effectively settled, when Genesee Fever attracted thousands to New York.[8] However one dates the beginning of this demographic trend, statistics show that Vermonters forsook their state in droves for greener pastures elsewhere.

The transportation industry cashed in on the stampede from Vermont. Typical of the enticements dangled before the public was the advertising by the Ogdensburg and Lake Champlain Railroad in 1884 that asked potential passengers from Windham County, the location of Jamaica, "Are You Going West?" The railroad declared itself to be the beginning leg of connections to all points in the Western states and territories, and tempted "parties seeking homes in the West" with promises of preferential treatment.[9]

Going West was only one of the demographic changes affecting Vermont. A population drift from the hills to urban centers and even villages also developed into a trend.[10] The *American Architect* disclosed in 1889 that 40,000 acres of formerly cultivated land lay abandoned in Windham County. Throughout the state, the number of deserted farms reached into the thousands.[11] It is a reasonable assumption that some of the former owners of these farms resettled in communities rather than moving to the West. Population losses in Jamaica reflected the state-wide trend of westward migration as well as the hemorrhaging in Windham County.

Seventh-day Adventists could not claim immunity to these realities. As early as 1856, E. L. Barr, a Sabbatarian pastor returning to Vermont after a year's absence, noted the "many vacant places caused by the saints' removing to the far West," either for spiritual or secular reasons.[12] In 1875, D. M. Canright, a visiting minister at the Adventist camp meeting in Essex Junction, observed that Vermont's Adventist population had suffered because many had moved to the West.[13]

Only days after arriving in Vermont in 1892 to assume pastoral duties, William Covert visited the Bordoville church, where he found that "death and removals" had reduced the congregation to about fifty. For years, before membership growth in Pikes Falls made it the largest church in Vermont, the Bordoville congregation had consistently reported the largest membership among Seventh-day Adventist churches in the state. Similarly, Covert complained in 1896 that "many removals" had ended the "work" in the northern community of Underhill, where he had just re-established a Sabbath school. One family had returned from the Adventist capital, Battle Creek, Michigan, prompting Covert to appeal to many others to "come back to these deserted churches."[14]

Church leaders linked their membership problems to the slow rate of Vermont's population increase—only 29,000 during the sixty years leading up to 1905—and, in turn, they blamed westward migration for Vermont's stunted growth. A. S. Hutchins guessed that during the forty years before 1893, some 1,500 Sabbath keepers from Vermont joined the exodus to the West.[15] A. C. Bourdeau was more conservative, estimating 1,000 Sabbath keepers had moved away from the state.[16] His slightly more charitable view of blame did not lessen the negative impact on the Vermont Conference.

Neither Hutchins nor Bourdeau was given to hyperbole. The numbers that they offered were only rough estimates, but they established a point. If a guess of 1,500, or even 1,000, was a fair approximation of membership losses in Vermont caused by members transferring outside the state, we can conclude that among Seventh-day Adventist conferences in the United States during the nineteenth century, Vermont was one of the most productive fields to convert new members. That the Vermont Conference reported only 532 members in 1900[17] was as much a tribute to the tenacity of church leaders as a commentary on slow membership growth.

We would be assuming the unlikely if we concluded that the Pikes Falls church escaped this demographic trend. Abbie Sage went to Michigan for an education and a teaching job but returned to Pikes Falls to die of tuberculosis. In 1905 several families connected to the Whites' mop wringer industry moved to the Erie Canal in New York. Likely, there were others. Isaac Pike assures us that the Pikes Falls community did, indeed, feel the impact of demographic movement. On March 15, 1869, he recorded in his diary that he "went up to Mr. Davidson's [the Lewis Davidson family] to see them start for the West."[18]

Seventh-day Adventist congregations were not the only ones who suffered from westward migration. Stilwell points out that "churches all over the state were losing members—some of them to the point of practical extinction."[19] This trend affected the economic well-being of the state and threatened the social fabric of Vermont. Discussing this point in the context of the uphill/downhill divide in Vermont, Paul Searls states that "the decline of many individual rural churches illustrated the decline of rural Vermont itself."[20]

Credit: Jamaica Historical Foundation

The White Mop Wringer Company, owned and operated by Cassius White, pictured sometime between 1895 and 1905. Of interest are the ladders leading up to the water barrels that perched on the roof.

Although Jamaica was a rural community, Mark Worthen aptly describes the town as a small but bustling nineteenth-century settlement and a center for trade and commerce in Windham County. An abbreviated economic dip followed the Civil War, he declares; however, in 1869, Jamaica was flourishing from the shops and mills that depended on power from several dams along the streams flowing through the community.[21] At this same time, A. C. Bourdeau was prodding the Seventh-day Adventist community to complete the construction of its meetinghouse.

But improvements in manufacturing and communication in the late nineteenth and early twentieth centuries inflicted serious damage on the industry that operated in Jamaica. The entrepreneurial ventures of Cassius White illustrate this point. Capitalizing on promising local conditions, he began a shingle and butter tub industry that morphed into a mop wringer enterprise, which, in turn, moved away after a more advantageous location beckoned from New York's Erie Canal.

The rise and decline of membership in the Adventist church in Jamaica corresponded to the economic fortunes of the town, but in delayed action. Despite its place on the periphery of the Vermont Conference, for years the congregation survived negative demographic and economic trends to become the largest Seventh-day Adventist congregation in the state and probably in the three states of northern New England. We may infer that spiritual motivation was stronger in drawing people to the church than were the influences that could have led them away. But during the first quarter of the twentieth century, the church's vulnerability to external conditions became irremediable. The resulting toll on membership eventually killed the church.

A Final Look at the Pikes Falls Congregation

The downward direction for the church appears to have set in early in the new century. When the meetinghouse closed its doors in the mid-1940s after more than seventy-five years as a place of worship, the population of the Jamaica township had dwindled to about a third of what it had been when A. S. Hutchins organized the first congregation in 1862.

While the overwhelming majority of the Pikes Falls church remain anonymous, the scattered facts about the few we know provide some insight about the rise, decline, and disappearance of the congregation. We cannot recreate the Seventh-day Adventist community by assuming that the families in this narrative were so typical of the rest of the congregation that they constitute a statistical control group through which to analyze the entire church, but we can legitimately generalize that they all faced the same conditions of weather, population shifts, economic change, and denominational influences.

We do not know how many of the congregation represented converts from the local population and how many moved to Jamaica from other places. The Sages, Pikes, Bourns, and Wilders were long-term residents of the area, but the Whites, Twings, and Dompiers moved to Pikes Falls. The Isaac Pike family descended from eighteenth-century settlers. The Hurds were not one of the original Sabbatarian families, but they had roots in the region. Floyd Hurd was born in Pikes Falls and was partly of Indian descent.[22] It is possible that the Twings had family ties to this part of Vermont.

When combined into a composite narrative, the stories of these families illustrate the truism that human experience constitutes a dynamic in which rising generations tend to push their horizons beyond their present range.

When combined into a composite narrative, the stories of these families illustrate the truism that human experience constitutes a dynamic in which rising generations tend to push their horizons beyond their present range. Despite the varying interpretations that historians have derived from the influences at work in Vermont's development, it is safe to say that seeking personal advantage was the underlying motivation that was common to all settlers in this state. Seeking personal advantage ran the gamut from land speculation and the desire to satisfy a craving for pioneer adventure on one hand, to the other end of the spectrum characterized by genuine attempts to establish a better life in a permanent setting.

With the passing of time, opening up new frontiers in the geographic sense of the word became a fading option. But no one could realistically expect that succeeding generations in Jamaica would always remain on the edge of the Green Mountains without looking elsewhere for more advantageous opportunities. The urge that drove Jamaica's new generations to move on to what they perceived to be better things was akin to the same spirit that had brought their forebears to Vermont in the first place.

Besides the general appeal of economic opportunity, Seventh-day Adventists experienced their own version of the desire to respond to advantages elsewhere. As a people, they retained the driving force of Millerism, a conviction that Christians were to spread the gospel of salvation throughout the world. Compelled by that conviction, former Millerites brought Sabbatarianism to Jamaica in 1852, which eventually gave rise to the church. This pattern of events repeated itself until the resulting congregations became a global movement. By the end of 1940, the world membership of Seventh-day Adventists edged beyond one-half million, 63 percent living outside North America.[23]

Seventh-day Adventist presses produced a copious flow of books and periodicals to inform both the church and the public about the advancement of their global undertakings. Church writers deliberately encouraged participation in this movement. Church educators also operated a worldwide network of schools, consistently maintaining that beyond the basic purpose of educating, one of their principal objectives was to prepare students for a role in denominational endeavors. Church members not only expected but also hoped that their young would choose a professional career, or at least a blue-collar position, in the employ of the church. Accordingly, Adventist parents commonly moved to locations where their children could more conveniently receive an education in denominational schools and enhance their opportunities to spend their lives in some phase of church work.

By definition, Seventh-day Adventists in Jamaica were part of this process. Typifying this tendency were some of the rising generations of the families in this study. Joseph Twing left for a career in teaching and preaching. His younger brother, James, became a physician and eventually entered mission service in Africa. J. G. White cut himself loose from a family business and worked in several locations in the United States as well as China.

The tradition of denominational service continued into future generations. Some of Isaac Pike's immediate descendants moved from Jamaica for personal reasons, but two of his great-grandsons trained to be ministers, both of them leading the pastoral district that included the Pikes Falls church. After her marriage, Joseph Dompier's youngest daughter, Abbie, worked with her husband for a short time at the denomination's medical center in Battle Creek, Michigan, before returning to Vermont. Their two daughters taught briefly in denominational elementary schools and one of their sons completed a lifetime career at a denominational sanitarium. Two of Dompier's great-grandchildren also had careers in church employment.[24] There are probably more from other Pikes Falls families whose names we could add to this list.

Although the congregation in Pikes Falls became large among Seventh-day Adventists in Vermont, New Hampshire, and Maine, its location was not conducive to becoming an enduring hub of denominational activity. New generations in the church felt not only the same economic pressures as everyone else to move, but compounding their feelings was their sense of loyalty to denominational goals, and they moved on to locations that were more active in church affairs. In short, as the twentieth century unfolded, for a combination of reasons, rising generations of Seventh-day Adventists found more justification to leave Jamaica than to remain. Similar to the compulsion that first attracted settlers to Vermont and then inspired them to leave, Adventists' commitment to a spiritual cause led them to the Jamaica church and also motivated them to move away.

Members may have had differing explanations as to why they gravitated to this remote nook in Vermont, but their connection with the church expressed their spiritual purposes, although at varying degrees. Jeremy Flaherty has concluded that religious relationships in Vermont deterred emigration, but his investigation also shows that influences produced outcomes that differed from one community to another.[25] We can only speculate that spiritual kinship held the Pikes Falls church together for years after economic decline began in Jamaica, and it also fostered growth. Ultimately, however, the forces that forged the church were no match against external trends. While the departure of members may have reflected spiritual purposes, morally neutral issues such as demographic and economic trends of the times also were part of the church's demise.

Finally, a related question asks how much the Seventh-day Adventist community contributed to the non-conformist reputation of Jamaica. The origins of the Pikes Falls church rest upon the experiences of Millerism that historians commonly categorize under the moniker of ultraism. We can inquire if the Pikes Falls church continued that ultraist mood.

Helen and Scott Nearing saw their Seventh-day Adventist neighbors as dedicated and committed people who would do "urgent chores" on Saturday, such as milk and feed their cattle, but otherwise "refused to work on Saturday or to do business that day."[26] The Nearings depict the contrasting definitions of "urgent chores" by experiences of the Walter Twing and the Hurd families, indicating that not all Seventh-day Adventists shared identical convictions, even about central doctrines of their church. But there was still room in the congregation for both families as members in good and regular standing.

The denomination advocated a progressively broadening range of health reform, including an endorsement of vegetarianism and simple diets, but these initiatives never became articles of faith. During the years when the Pikes Falls church existed, only abstinence from tobacco and alcohol were temperance-related tests of membership.[27] The Nearings also taught these same lifestyle health principles. Perhaps the mutual respect among the Twings, Hurds, and Nearings derived, in part, from their similar convictions.

> *The members of the Jamaica church sought to integrate themselves into the existing social order and contribute to the community's well-being.*

However different the members of the Pikes Falls church may have been from the public at large, the facts that we know about the families in this study do not tell a story of a separatist people or a colony isolating itself within the walls of its own utopia. Rather, the members of the Jamaica church sought to integrate themselves into the existing social order and contribute to the community's well-being.

Before becoming a Sabbatarian, Isaac Pike's participation in community affairs spoke for itself as did his neighbors' acceptance of his Thomsonian practice of medicine. That he continued to participate in public life after becoming a Sabbatarian is not surprising. Cassius White established himself as a respected businessman and inventor by operating a prosperous enterprise that brought money to Jamaica's slipping economy. Some members of the Seventh-day Adventist community held public offices, serving in both the Stratton and Jamaica townships as selectman, road supervisor, town clerk, town lister, grand juryman, district school leader, and town treasurer.

Both Floyd Hurd and his father represented Stratton in the Vermont General Assembly. Seventh-day Adventists differed from other Christians by preaching a premillennial second advent, worshipping on a different day, and practicing health reform, but these differences did not prevent the Methodist church in Bondville or the Congregational church in Jamaica from requesting O. O. Farnsworth to become their temporary pastor. The Pikes Falls Seventh-day Adventists were not the same people as their Millerite antecedents whom angry onlookers stoned and shot at in 1844.

The story of the Seventh-day Adventist Church in Jamaica demonstrates one of Jeffrey Potash's underlying themes in *Vermont's Burned-Over District,* the truth that congregations do not exist in isolation from their environments. While our limited knowledge about the families we have met in this study enables us to offer only calculated guesses about the congregation itself, the known experiences of Seventh-day Adventists in Pikes Falls illustrate the fact that if churches are committed to ideals that are quintessentially other-worldly, the environments in which they function and their immediate pursuits are inherently mundane. It is only natural for church members to react to both.

Eventually, the Pikes Falls church succumbed to its environment, but Seventh-day Adventists who had experienced the old Jamaica did not reject their heritage. The regional meetings in the old meetinghouse, especially the visit by D. A. Ochs in 1942, led contemporaries and survivors of earlier generations on journeys of nostalgic reminiscence. These gatherings were often emotional reminders that the success of modern Seventh-day Adventism was rooted in the hardihood of the church's past. To cultivate a deliberate consciousness of this legacy was also a part of Seventh-day Adventist tradition.

The narrative of the Seventh-day Adventist community in Jamaica may be only a footnote in the larger story of how a strand of Millerism evolved into a major denomination, and how a single congregation reflected broader economic and demographic developments in Vermont. Not only does this local history convey lessons to the Seventh-day Adventist Church at large, but it also is a reminder of the importance of small details in the past, nearly forgotten in the sweep of time, that bring meaning to our ever-changing present.

Notes

1. *Yearbook* for the years 1894–1909. See sections, "Vermont Conference."
2. "Vermont, Rutland, Manchester, Bennington, Jamaica," *Gleaner*, June 15, 1904; *Yearbook*, 1904, p. 20.
3. Trace the organizational changes and the migration of conference offices in *Yearbook*, 1909–1927.
4. *Yearbook*, 1910–1920. So scarce were ministers during this period that elected lay members instead of ministers headed many conference activities.
5. *Statistical Report of Seventh-day Adventist Conferences, Missions, and Institutions for the Year Ending December 31, 1910;* ibid., 1940. The General Conference published annual statistical reports under different titles, but they are all known by the generic term *Statistical Report*.

6. See US Census, Vermont Genealogy Resources, http://1ref.us/hd (accessed July 17, 2012).
7. F. W. Beers, *Atlas of Windham Co. Vermont* (New York, 1869). Helen and Scott Nearing helped to organize a community campaign against the Postal Service. Washington caved in after negative publicity went nationwide. See Nearing, *Good Life*, pp. 182–185.
8. Stilwell, *Emigration From Vermont*, pp. 120, 135.
9. *Gazetteer*, p. 609.
10. Michael Sherman, Gene Sessions, and P. Jeffrey Potash, *Freedom and Unity: A History of Vermont* (Barre, VT: Vermont Historical Society, 2004), pp. 167, 288–290, 515; Stilwell, *Emigration From Vermont*, pp. 120, 121. For continued population shifts westward, see Stilwell's discussion beginning on page 124; Barkun, *Crucible*, pp. 104–106.
11. *American Architect* in "Go East, Young Man," cited in *RH*, November 12, 1889.
12. "From Bro. Barr," *RH*, January 8, 1857.
13. "Vermont Camp-Meeting," *RH*, September 2, 1875.
14. "Vermont," *RH*, October 11, 1892; "Vermont," *RH*, February 11, 1896.
15. "Biennial Report of the Vermont Conference, Ending August 31, 1905," *Gleaner*, November 20, 1905.
16. "Vermont," *RH*, June 13, 1893.
17. General Conference Bulletin, 1900.
18. Pike Diary, March 15.
19. Stilwell, *Emigration From Vermont*, p. 224.
20. Searls, *Two Vermonts*, p. 88.
21. Worthen, *Hometown Jamaica*, pp. 40–52.
22. Nearing, *Good Life*, p. 93; Elizabeth Hurd Greene, telephone interview by Floyd Greenleaf, October 1, 2012.
23. *Statistical Report*, 1940.
24. Tracing the Pike family has been documented elsewhere in this book. Besides archival sources, I have relied on personal knowledge to verify the references about the Dompier family.
25. Jeremy Flaherty, "A Multivariate Look at Migration from Vermont," *Vermont History* (Summer/Fall 2006), pp. 127–155.
26. Nearing, *Good Life*, p. 172.
27. Malcolm Bull and Keith Lockhart have concluded that Seventh-day Adventist emphasis on health reform has been its most striking attribute aside from its doctrinal positions. See Bull and Lockhart, *Seeking a Sanctuary: Seventh-day Adventism and the American Dream*, 2nd ed., (Bloomington: Indiana University Press, 2007), pp. 11–17.

Health reform was absent from the statement of beliefs that Seventh-day Adventists issued in 1872. Article 17 of a new statement of beliefs that appeared in 1931 stipulated that the "believer will be led to abstain from all intoxicating drinks, tobacco, and other narcotics, and the avoidance of every body- and soul-defiling habit and practice." In 1980 the church added "unclean foods identified in the Scriptures" to their dietary prohibitions. See a verbatim comparison of the denomination's three successive statements of beliefs in Gary Land, *Adventism in America* (Grand Rapids: William B. Eerdmans Publishing Company, 1986), pp. 231–250.

Bibliography

Books and Reference Works

Barkun, Michael. *Crucible of the Millennium.* Syracuse, NY: Syracuse University Press, 1986.

Bassett, T. D. Seymour, *The Gods of the Hills.* Montpelier: Vermont Historical Society, 2000.

Beers, F. W., *Atlas of Windham Co. Vermont.* New York, 1869.

------, *Atlas of Windham Co. Vermont.* Centennial Edition. 1869–1969.

Bliss, Sylvester. *Memoirs of William Miller.* Boston: Joshua V. Himes, 1853.

Booker, Warren E., ed. *Historical Notes: Jamaica, Windham County, Vermont.* Brattleboro: E. L. Hildreath & Co., 1940.

Boutelle, Luther. *Sketch of the Life and Religious Experience of Eld. Luther Boutelle.* Boston: Advent Christian Publication Society, 1891.

Bright, Jean Hay. *Meanwhile, Next Door to the Good Life.* Dixmont, ME; BrightBerry Press, 2003.

Bull, Malcolm, and Keith Lockhart. *Seeking a Sanctuary: Seventh-day Adventism and the American Dream*, 2nd ed. Bloomington: Indiana University Press, 2007.

Child, Hamilton, ed., *Gazetteer and Business Directory of Windham County, Vt., 1724–1884*. Syracuse, NY: Journal Office, 1884.

Crocker, Henry. *History of the Baptists in Vermont*. Bellows Falls, VT: P. H. Gobie Press, 1913.

Cross, Whitney R. *The Burned-Over District*. Ithaca, NY: Cornell University Press, 1950.

Dick, Everett N., and Gary Land. *William Miller and the Advent Crisis*. Berrien Springs, MI: Andrews University Press, 1994.

Doan, Ruth Alden. *Miller Heresy, Millennialism, and American Culture*. Philadelphia: Temple University Press, 1987.

Fortin, Denis. *Adventism in Quebec*. Berrien Springs, MI: Andrews University Press, 2004.

Hemenway, Abby Maria, ed. *Vermont Historical Gazetteer*. 5 vols. Various publishing houses in Vermont, 1867–1891. Citations from this source are listed under the names of the contributors.

Jetté, René. *Dictionnaire Généalogique des Familles du Québec*. Montreal: Les Presses de l'Université de Montreal, 1983.

Joly, Greg, and Rebecca Lepkoff. *Almost Utopia: The Residents and Radicals of Pikes Falls, Vermont, 1950*. Barre, VT: Vermont Historical Society, 2008.

Journal of the General Assembly of the State of Vermont for the Session Begun in 1835. Middlebury, VT: Knapp and Jewett, 1835.

Knight, George R. *Millennial Fever and the End of the World*. Nampa, ID: Pacific Press Publishing Association, 1993.

Land, Gary, ed. *Adventism in America*. Grand Rapids: William B. Eerdmans Publishing Company, 1986.

Ludlum, David M. *Social Ferment in Vermont*. New York: Columbia University Press, 1939.

Maxwell, C. Mervyn. *Magnificent Disappointment*. Nampa, ID: Pacific Press Publishing Association, 1994.

McMaster, John Bach. *A History of the People of the United States, From the Revolution to the Civil War.* Vol. 7. New York: D. Appleton and Company, 1920.

Nearing, Helen and Scott. *The Good Life.* New York: Schocken Books, Inc. 1989. This edition contains two of the Nearings' books: *Living the Good Life.* Harborside, ME: Social Science Institute, 1954; and *Continuing the Good Life.* New York: Schocken Books, Inc., 1979.

------. *The Maple Sugar Book.* 50th-anniversary edition. White River Junction, VT: Chelsea Green Publishing Company, 2000. Originally published in 1950 by John Day Co.

Nichol, F. D. *The Midnight Cry.* Washington, D.C.: Review and Herald Publishing Association, 1944.

Numbers, Ronald L. *Prophetess of Health: A Study of Ellen G. White.* New York: Harper and Row, 1976.

Numbers, Ronald L. and Jonathan M. Butler, eds. *The Disappointed.* Knoxville: University of Tennessee Press, 1993. Citations from this source are listed under the names of the contributors.

Potash, P. Jeffrey. *Vermont's Burned-Over District.* Brooklyn: Carlson Publishing Inc., 1991.

Rivest, Lucien. *Mariages du Comté de l'Assomption.* Montreal: Quintin Publications, 1972.

Roth, Randolph A. *The Democratic Dilemma.* Cambridge: Cambridge University Press, 1987.

Rowe, David. *Thunder and Trumpets.* Chico, CA: Scholars Press, 1985.

Searls, Paul M. *Two Vermonts: Geography and Identity, 1865–1910.* Durham, NH: University of New Hampshire Press, 2006.

Sears, Clara Endicott. *Days of Delusion.* Boston: Houghton Mifflin Company, 1924.

Seventh-day Adventist Encyclopedia. 2nd rev. ed. 2 vols. Hagerstown, MD: Review and Herald Publishing Association, 1996.

Sherman, Michael, Gene Sessions, and P. Jeffrey Potash. *Freedom and Unity: A History of Vermont.* Barre, VT: Vermont Historical Society, 2004.

St-Henri de Mascouche, comté de L'Assomption, 1750–1993. Joliette, Québec: Société de généalogie de Lanaudière, 2000.

Stilwell, Lewis D. *Emigration From Vermont*. Montpelier, VT: Vermont Historical Society, 1948.

Tanguay, Cyprien. *Dictionnaire Généalogique des Familles Canadiennes*. Québec: Eusèbe Senécal, 1871–1890.

Tyler, Alice Felt. *Freedom's Ferment*. Minneapolis: University of Minnesota Press, 1944.

Vande Vere, Emmet K. *Rugged Heart: The Story of George I. Butler*. Nashville, TN: Southern Publishing Association, 1979.

Wellcome, Isaac C. *History of the Second Advent Message and Mission, Doctrine and People*. Yarmouth, ME: I. C. Wellcome, 1874.

White, Arthur L. White. *Ellen G. White*. 6 vols. Hagerstown, MD: Review and Herald Publishing Association, 1981–1986. Individual titles of specific volumes are used in the notes for specific citations.

White, Ellen G. *Testimonies for the Church*. 9 vols. Mountain View, CA: Pacific Press Publishing Association, 1948.

Worthen, Mark. *Hometown Jamaica*. Brattleboro, VT: Griswold Offset Printing Inc., 1976.

Young, D. K. *Echoes in the Forest*. Stratton: Town of Stratton: 2000.

------. *The History of Stratton*. Stratton: Town of Stratton, 2001.

Articles

Altherr, Thomas L. "A Convention of 'Moral Lunatics': The Rutland, Vermont, Free Convention of 1858." *Vermont History* (Winter 2001, Symposium Supplement), pp. 90-104.

Erlich, James. "Ascension Robes and Other Millerite Fables." *Adventist Heritage* (Summer 1975), pp. 8–13.

Flaherty, Jeremy. "A Multivariate Look at Migration from Vermont." *Vermont History* (Summer/Fall 2006), pp. 127–155.

McReynolds, Samuel A. "Frontiers to Farms, to Factories: The Economic and Social Development of Vermont from 1791 to 1991." *Vermont History* (winter/spring 2003), pp. 88–97.

Parker, Jane Marsh. "Did the Millerites Have Ascension Robes?" *The Outlook*. October 13, 1894, pp. 582, 583.

Roth, Randolph. "Can Faith Change the World? Religion and Society in Vermont's Age of Reform." *Vermont History* (Winter 2001, Symposium Supplement), pp. 7–18.

Scharnhorst, Gary. "Images of the Millerites in American Literature." *American Quarterly* (Spring 1980), pp. 19–36.

Senécal, Joseph-André. "'Nos Ancêtres les Gaulois': Ethnicity and History in Vermont." *Vermont History* (Winter/Spring 2003), pp. 62–70.

Sprague, John Francis Sprague. "The Millerites in Maine." *Sprague's Journal of Maine History* (January, February, March 1922), pp. 1–6.

Wait, Gary E. "The End of the World." *Dartmouth College Library Bulletin* (November 1993), p. 7. http://1ref.us/he (accessed April 8, 2012).

Periodicals

Acts and Resolves Passed by the General Assembly of the State of Vermont at the October Session, 1856

Advent Review and Sabbath Herald

Annual Report of the Commissioner of Patents

Atlantic Union Gleaner

Evening Recorder (Amsterdam, NY)

Free Press (Burlington, VT)

General Conference Bulletin

Health Reformer

Pacific Union Recorder

Seventh-day Adventist Yearbook

Statistical Report of Seventh-day Adventist Conferences, Missions, and Institutions. Variations in the title of this annual report appear from year to year. The most commonly used name for the report is *Statistical Report*.

Manuscripts, Archival Materials, and Unpublished Studies

Les Archives Nationales du Québec. Parish records from these archives as reproduced and stored in American-French Genealogical libraries in Burlington, Vermont, and Woonsocket, Rhode Island.

Crocombe, Jeff. "'A Feast of Reason': The Roots of William Miller's Biblical Interpretation and Its Influence on the Seventh-day Adventist Church." PhD dissertation. University of Queensland, Australia, 2011.

Gurdon Hibbard Farm Diary and Account Book. Vermont Historical Library. Barre, VT.

General Conference Committee Minutes, available online by Office of Archives, Statistics, and Research, General Conference of Seventh-day Adventists, Silver Spring, MD. http://1ref.us/hf (accessed January 31, 2017).

History of the Pikes Falls Church, no author, no date. Authorship of this single-page note attributed to a member of the Isaac Pike family, but Flavius White is named as the owner of the document.

Isaac Pike Diary, 1869. Charles Marchant, owner.

Letter. George I. Butler to Ellen G. White. January 28, 1904. Ellen G. White Estate (General Conference of Seventh-day Adventists: Silver Spring, MD).

Town Records of Jamaica, VT.

Town Records of Stratton, VT.

United States Census records.

Vermont Vital Records.

Ward, Donal. "Religious Enthusiasm in Vermont, 1761–1847." PhD dissertation. Notre Dame University, 1980.

TEACH Services, Inc.
PUBLISHING

We invite you to view the complete
selection of titles we publish at:
www.TEACHServices.com

We encourage you to write us
with your thoughts about this,
or any other book we publish at:
info@TEACHServices.com

TEACH Services' titles may be purchased in
bulk quantities for educational, fund-raising,
business, or promotional use.
bulksales@TEACHServices.com

Finally, if you are interested in seeing
your own book in print, please contact us at:
publishing@TEACHServices.com

We are happy to review your manuscript at no charge.

www.ingramcontent.com/pod-product-compliance
Lightning Source LLC
Chambersburg PA
CBHW070542170426
43200CB00011B/2515